Successful Strategies
for Reading in the
Content Areas

2nd Edition

SHELL EDUCATION

Successful Strategies
for Reading in the Content Areas
2nd Edition
Grades 3–5

Editor
Conni Medina

Assistant Editor
Leslie Huber, M.A.

Senior Editor
Lori Kamola, M.S.Ed.

Editor-in-Chief
Sharon Coan, M.S.Ed.

Editorial Manager
Gisela Lee, M.A.

Creative Director
Lee Aucoin

Cover Design
Neri Garcia

Imaging
Sandra Riley
Don Tran

Authors
TCM Staff

Publisher
Corinne Burton, M.A.Ed.

Shell Education
5301 Oceanus Drive
Huntington Beach, CA 92649
http://www.shelleducation.com
ISBN 978-1-4258-0469-5

©2008 Shell Education
Made in U.S.A.

Table of Contents

Introduction

The saying "Every teacher is a teacher of reading" is well known but not always true. It is usually regarded as the task of the English or language arts teacher to guide students through the effective use of comprehension strategies as they read. Although students read in almost every subject area they study, content-area teachers typically overlook the need for guiding students through their textbook-based and trade book-based reading tasks. Comprehension strategies best serve students when they are employed across the curricula and in the context of their actual learning. It is only then that students can independently use the strategies successfully when reading. Students typically read literature or fictional stories for English or language arts, but they will spend the majority of their adulthood reading nonfiction, expository writing. The strategies that students use to comprehend literature are different from those they use for nonfiction. It is important to note that around grades four and five educators see a drop in reading achievement. At this time, students seem to lose interest in reading independently, spend less time reading for pleasure, and struggle more to read the materials required of them at school. It is for this reason that all teachers at all levels must actively pursue ways to greatly enhance their students' ability to understand reading material, and this can be accomplished by working directly with reading comprehension strategies.

How to Use This Book

Reading comprehension is a complex process involving interactions between the reader and the text, using multiple skills. Students need a variety of strategies to be successful readers. *Successful Strategies for Reading in the Content Areas,* 2nd Edition contains a variety of reading strategies that will help increase comprehension. This updated edition has grouped the strategies and skills to match the seven categories of strategies and skills taught in *Exploring Nonfiction: A Differentiated Content-Area Reading Program* (Teacher Created Materials Publishing 2008). An additional section, titled Developing Vocabulary, is also provided in this book. This book is divided into the following sections:

- **Monitor Comprehension** (including **Set the Purpose** and **Author's Point of View**)
- **Activate and Connect**
- **Infer Meaning**
- **Ask Questions**
- **Determine Importance** (including **Main Idea and Supporting Details, Text Structures, Text Organizers,** and **Using Parts of the Book**)
- **Visualize**
- **Summarize and Synthesize**
- **Developing Vocabulary**

Introduction

How to Use This Book *(cont.)*

Each of these eight sections contains an introduction, teaching strategies, and reproducible templates for students. Many of the teaching strategies have corresponding graphic organizers or other templates included, with page number references to direct you to the correct reproducible page. It is important to read the introduction to each section before using the strategies to understand how best to teach these important nonfiction skills. For further information, and to understand the research about reading comprehension and content-area reading, read the rest of this introduction. You will also find a Correlation to Standards chart (pages 14–16) showing the national standards to which each strategy is aligned. A CD is provided at the back of this book with all of the graphic organizers and templates in PDF format so you can print them. Most of these pages are also provided in Microsoft Word so that they can be modified. An index of these pages is provided on the CD.

This book provides a wealth of information about content-area reading strategies and skills that can be used with any nonfiction text. The strategies and skills can also be used in conjunction with *Exploring Nonfiction: A Differentiated Content-Area Reading Program* as a resource guide to support the lesson plans. Refer to the Works Cited (page 276) for a list of references used to create this book.

Research: Explicit Instruction of Reading Comprehension Strategies

If content-area teachers were asked how they improve their students' reading skills, the majority would most likely struggle to answer the question. Good teachers use many strategies to enhance students' reading comprehension, and it is helpful to identify which strategies they use in order to explain why the techniques successfully improve their students' skills. Even more important is the explicit instruction of the individual strategies, including modeling, guided practice, and independent practice. These steps ensure that students learn to independently and consistently use a wide variety of reading comprehension strategies for a broad range of reading experiences.

Teaching students the strategies to improve their comprehension is nothing new to educators. Extensive research has demonstrated that students greatly benefit from the direct instruction of reading comprehension strategies when reading a text (Duke and Pearson 2002; Block 1999; Dole, Brown, and Trathen 1996; Durkin 1978; Pressley and Afflerbach 1995, as cited by Kragler, Walker, and Martin 2005). Simply put, strategy instruction is an effective means of assisting students in improving comprehension and understanding. This book, *Successful Strategies for Reading in the Content Areas*, is designed to give content-area teachers tools for teaching reading comprehension strategies.

Introduction

Research: Which Strategies to Teach

The National Reading Panel Report (2000), commissioned by the U.S. Congress to evaluate research in the area of reading, identified a number of effective comprehension strategies. Pressley (2000) echoes these findings. These strategies include vocabulary development, prediction skills (including inference), the building of prior knowledge, think-alouds, visual representations, summarization, and questioning. This book provides an explanation of these strategies and describes a number of activities that content-area teachers can incorporate into their lessons. These findings guide the selection of strategies included in *Successful Strategies for Reading in the Content Areas.*

Students also need to develop their metacognitive skills when reading and learning. Scholars agree that metacognition plays a significant role in reading comprehension (e.g., Baker and Brown 1984; Garner 1987; Mastropieri and Scruggs 1997; Paris, Wasik, and Turner 1991; Schraw 1998, as cited by Baker 2002). Research shows that teachers should foster metacognition and comprehension monitoring during comprehension instruction because in doing so, students will be able to monitor and self-regulate their ability to read. "Developing engaged readers involves helping students to become both strategic and aware of the strategies they use to read" (McCarthy, Hoffman, and Galda 1999, as cited by Baker 2002).

It is important to note that teachers should never take a "one size fits all" approach when teaching reading comprehension. Some strategies work for some students, and other strategies work for other students, just as some strategies work best with certain types of reading material, and other strategies work best with other types of reading material. The most important thing to remember when trying to improve reading comprehension in students is that the skill level, group dynamic, and makeup of the students should determine the approach to take.

Research: The Steps Involved in Explicit Instruction of Reading Comprehension Strategies

According to Duke and Pearson (2002), research supports that a balanced approach to teaching reading comprehension is more than teaching students specific reading strategies and providing opportunities to read. Teachers should begin with direct explanation and instruction of how to use the strategies so that after a series of steps, students will be able to use the strategies independently. The following are the five steps for explicit instruction of comprehension strategies:

1. **Provide an exact description of the strategy and explain when and how it should be used.** Teachers need to explain what the strategy is called, why students should use it, what it helps them understand, and how often students should use it.

2. **Provide modeling of the strategy.** Teachers should model how to use the strategy when students are in the process of reading. Students can also model the strategy while the teacher reinforces an explanation of how the strategy is being used.

3. **Provide opportunities for collaborative use of the strategy in action.** Teachers and students should work together and share their use of the strategy while they are reading.

4. **Lead guided practice sessions using the strategy, and allow for a gradual release of responsibility from the teacher to the student.** At this stage, teachers can remind students of how to use the strategy and of the steps involved, but teachers should allow students to work on the technique independently.

5. **Encourage students' independent use of the strategy.** In the final stage, teachers might gently remind students of the name of the strategy, but the students should be using the technique automatically and independently.

Duke and Pearson (2002) emphasize the importance of remembering that students need to be able to use more than one comprehension strategy to understand a reading selection. Throughout the five phases, other strategies should be referenced and modeled for the students. When working with reading materials in any content area, teachers should use the very same techniques to introduce a new learning strategy to students as they would during language arts or in an English class. Research shows that students can master the use of reading comprehension strategies when instruction follows the five steps listed above. When covering any topic, teachers must take the time to allow students to master the strategy so that they can become independent readers. Follow these steps with the strategies in this book, and students will improve their comprehension.

Introduction

Research: What Great Teachers Do

Many content-area teachers use a variety of strategies that go beyond simply answering the questions at the end of the chapter. Research shows, however, that there is a big difference between teaching reading comprehension strategies well and teaching them in a dynamic, ingenious way that motivates and excites students about reading and learning. Through research, observations, and conversations with teachers who have been successful with the direct instruction of reading comprehension strategies, Keene (2002) has identified five traits specific to outstanding and consistently effective teachers. What makes these teachers effective?

1. **They take the time to understand each strategy in their own reading.** Reading about the techniques and activities is not enough. Great teachers of reading comprehension strategies take the time to figure out how to use and understand every strategy with the texts they are reading. In doing so, they increase their own metacognitive skills and can better articulate their own thinking during reading.

2. **They incorporate reading comprehension strategy instruction into predictable daily, weekly, and monthly activities.** Effective teachers of reading comprehension strategies set goals for strategy learning and create a predictable schedule to ensure that those goals are met. These teachers also set aside time to work more intensively with small groups as needed. They also set aside time for students to reflect on their progress toward the goals they set.

3. **They ask students to apply each comprehension strategy to a wide variety of texts and text levels in different contexts.** Great teachers use beautifully written texts with challenging and profound themes that can be read in their entirety in a mini-lesson. For example, they ask students to summarize the textbook and a short story, to use sensory images in poetry and expository essays, and to use background knowledge to understand a biography and the letters to the editor. In order to comprehend actively and assertively, students must read from texts with appropriately challenging words and concepts.

4. **They vary the size of groupings for strategy instruction.** Changing the group size and configuration helps teachers focus on different goals during comprehension strategy instruction.

   Large groups are best for:
   - introducing a new strategy
   - modeling think-alouds to show students how good readers use the strategy
   - practicing think-alouds with new genres, and allowing students to share their experiences using the strategy

Research: What Great Teachers Do *(cont.)*

Small groups are best for:

- providing more intensive instruction for students who need it
- introducing gifted students to the strategy so that they can apply it independently to more challenging texts and to new genres
- introducing new activities that enable students to share their thinking (new maps, charts, thinking notebooks, sketches, logs, etc.)
- allowing students to discuss books and comprehension strategies without teacher involvement

Conferences are best for:

- checking the student's understanding of how to apply the strategy he or she is studying to his or her own books
- providing intensive strategy instruction to a text that may be particularly challenging to the student
- coaching a student in how he or she might reveal his or her thinking to others
- pushing a student to use a strategy to think more deeply than he or she might have imagined possible

5. **They gradually release the responsibility for the application of a comprehension strategy to the students.** Great teachers follow the steps involved in the explicit instruction of reading comprehension strategies (Duke and Pearson 2002): over several weeks, teachers provide thorough explanations of the strategy, model how to use it, allow for group work with the strategy, transition to more independent use, and then release the responsibility to the students.

By following these guidelines for the teacher and using the strategies in this book, students will be provided with rich and meaningful opportunities for comprehension instruction.

Introduction

Research: What Do Good Readers Do When They Read?

Duke and Pearson (2002) have established that good readers:

- read actively

- set goals for their reading tasks and constantly evaluate whether the text and their reading of it is meeting their goals

- preview the text prior to reading, noting the text organization and structure in order to locate the sections most relevant to their reading goals

- make predictions about what is to come in the text

- read selectively, continually making decisions about their reading process: what to read carefully, what to read quickly, what to skim, what not to read, and what to reread

- construct, revise, and question the meanings they develop as they read

- determine the meanings of unfamiliar or unknown words and concepts in the text

- draw from, compare, and integrate their prior knowledge with the material in the text

- consider the authors of the text, their style, beliefs, intentions, historical perspective, and so on

- monitor their understanding of the text, make adjustments in their reading as necessary, and deal with inconsistencies or gaps as needed

- evaluate the text's quality and value, and interact with the text in multiple ways, both intellectually and emotionally

- read different kinds of texts differently

- construct and revise summaries of what they have read when reading expository texts

- think about the text before, during, and after reading

- feel satisfied and productive when reading, even though comprehension is a consuming, continuous, and complex activity

Content-area teachers can easily incorporate the same techniques that language arts teachers have used for years to help students become more strategic and skilled readers and to help them comprehend the materials they encounter. Teachers will find the job of using the textbook much easier if every student has the skills of a good reader.

Opportunities for all of the activities above are provided in the strategies listed throughout this book.

Introduction

Research: The Reading Process

Teachers need to understand the steps of the reading process in order to help students improve their reading comprehension skills. Content-area teachers can easily optimize the use of reading materials with students by utilizing the three-part framework of the reading process to facilitate learning. Break reading assignments into three comprehension-building steps: before reading, during reading, and after reading (Pressley 2002). It is important to note that what teachers do during each stage of the reading process is crucial to their students' learning.

Before Reading

Prior to beginning a reading assignment, engage in a variety of activities in the hopes of reducing any uncertainty involved in the reading task. These activities include generating interest in the topic, building and activating prior knowledge, and setting the purpose for reading.

Teachers who motivate students and create interest prior to assigning the reading improve their students' overall comprehension. Students who are more motivated to read are more engaged and actively involved in the process of learning than those who are not motivated. Motivated readers are also more likely to have better long-term recall of what they read.

Teachers can motivate students by assessing their prior knowledge. Knowing students' background knowledge on a topic makes it easier to build on and activate that knowledge during reading. The mind holds information in the form of frameworks called *schemata*, and as we learn new information, we store it in a framework of what we already know. Teachers who build on and activate students' prior knowledge before reading prepare students to more efficiently comprehend the material that they will be reading.

Prior to reading, teachers should prepare students to read by setting a purpose for the reading task. There are a number of different purposes a student can have for a reading assignment: predict what will happen, learn new vocabulary, summarize the information, evaluate the author's point of view, and so on. Students need to know what their purpose is as they read because it helps them to focus their efforts. In doing so, teachers can guide the students' search for meaning as they read.

Teachers should also take the time to introduce key concepts and vocabulary prior to reading. In doing so, they help the students to read the selection more fluently, with greater automaticity, and with greater comprehension, all of which lead to greater recall of the information.

Finally, teachers should establish in their students a metacognitive awareness for the task of reading. Students should be prompted to be aware of what they are thinking and doing as they are reading. Developing metacognitive awareness allows students to better understand the strategies necessary for effective learning. It also enables students to take control of their own learning and makes them more independent readers and learners.

Introduction

The Reading Process *(cont.)*

During Reading

During reading, students are actively reading text aloud or silently. During this stage of the reading process, students are engaged in answering questions (either self-generated or teacher-generated), monitoring their comprehension of the text, clarifying the purpose of reading, visualizing the information, and building connections.

Most often, students are engaged in answering questions while they read. Proficient readers self-question as they read to make sure they understand the reading material. In addition, students search for the answers to questions they may have generated prior to reading. As students process the text, they begin to infer what the author intended, and they begin to generalize about the specific details in the information provided. They also look for support for the predictions they have made.

Students are involved in monitoring and regulating their reading abilities while they are actively reading. If a section of the text is confusing, students need to know that they can reread the section, use fix-up strategies to help them understand what they are puzzled by, or adjust the speed of reading to suit their purposes and to suit the difficulty of the text. Thus, students must monitor their own reading strategies and make modifications as needed.

In addition to monitoring their reading abilities, students are also figuring out words as they actively read. If they do not know what a word means, they use the context clues or word parts to decode the meaning of the word. As students attend to vocabulary needs, they also observe the text structure and features as they read, which helps them organize the new information while they read.

During reading, teachers can focus students' attention on the objectives of the reading task. Students may adjust their purposes for reading based on the information they are reading and on their prior knowledge.

Proficient readers actively work to create images in their mind that represent the concepts in the reading material. Teachers should engage the students in creating mental images to help them comprehend the material as they are reading. This promotes greater recall of the information and engages the students in the reading process.

While students are reading, they are in the process of connecting the new information they are learning to their existing schemata. Therefore, teachers should be actively involved in helping students make connections between what they already know and what they are learning. This prepares them for the synthesis of the information. Teachers can be instrumental in helping students relate to the material.

Introduction

The Reading Process *(cont.)*

After Reading

Students expand their understanding of the material after reading the text. During the final stage of the reading process, students build connections among the bits of information that they have read, enabling them to deepen their understanding and reflect on what they have learned.

After reading, students need the teacher to guide them through follow-up experiences so they can reflect on what they have read. During reflection, students can contemplate the new information, clarify new ideas, refine their thinking, and connect what they have learned to other ideas to synthesize the new information. Teachers should spend time revisiting the text with students to demonstrate that the reading experience is not a single event.

Also, students generally find the main idea and distinguish the most important ideas from less important ideas. This enables them to prioritize and summarize what they have read.

After reading, teachers generally assess what students have learned. Students answer questions about what they have learned, and teachers generally use their answers to determine whether or not the students can move on or need additional instruction. Teachers can take advantage of additional activities for after reading to deepen students' comprehension of the text.

After students have read, they are able to engage in higher-level thinking tasks. Students can use critical thinking to evaluate the quality or validity of the material, or they can synthesize what they have learned by integrating their new knowledge with their prior knowledge. They can also analyze what they have read by closely examining the text characteristics specific to the genre.

Introduction

Correlation to Standards

The No Child Left Behind (NCLB) legislation mandates that all states adopt academic standards that identify the skills students will learn in kindergarten through grade 12. While many states had already adopted academic standards prior to NCLB, the legislation set requirements to ensure the standards were detailed and comprehensive.

Standards are designed to focus instruction and guide adoption of curricula. Standards are statements that describe the criteria necessary for students to meet specific academic goals. They define the knowledge, skills, and content students should acquire at each level. Standards are also used to develop standardized tests to evaluate students' academic progress.

In many states today, teachers are required to demonstrate how their lessons meet state standards. State standards are used in the development of Shell Education products, so educators can be assured that they meet the academic requirements of each state.

How to Find Your State Correlations

Shell Education is committed to producing educational materials that are research- and standards-based. In this effort, all products are correlated to the academic standards of the 50 states, the District of Columbia, and the Department of Defense Dependent Schools. A correlation report customized for your state can be printed directly from the following website: **http://www.shelleducation.com**. If you require assistance in printing correlation reports, please contact Customer Service at 1-800-877-3450.

McREL Compendium

Shell Education uses the Mid-continent Research for Education and Learning (McREL) Compendium to create standards correlations. Each year, McREL analyzes state standards and revises the compendium. By following this procedure, McREL is able to produce a general compilation of national standards.

Each reading comprehension strategy assessed in this book is based on one or more McREL content standards. The chart on pages 15–16 shows the McREL standards that correlate to each strategy provided in the book.

Introduction

Correlation to Standards *(cont.)*

Standard/Objective	Page (Strategy)
5.1—Previews text (e.g., skims material; uses pictures, textual clues, and text format)	22(6); 63(1, 2, 4); 64(5, 6, 7); 65(9); 112(12); 128(1); 133(8); 134(9); 171(1); 191(10); 212(2, 3); 215(16); 216(17); 236(11)
5.2—Establishes a purpose for reading (e.g., for information, for pleasure, to understand a specific viewpoint)	21(1, 2, 3); 22(4, 5, 6, 7); 23(8, 9, 10); 24(15); 189(2); 190(3, 4); 191(10, 11)
5.3—Makes, confirms, and revises simple predictions about what will be found in a text (e.g., uses prior knowledge and ideas presented in text, illustrations, titles, topic sentences, key words, and foreshadowing clues)	63(1); 64(7); 65(8); 66(12); 87(9); 172(5); 255(1)
5.4—Uses phonetic and structural analysis techniques, syntactic structure, and semantic context to decode unknown words (e.g., vowel patterns, complex word families, syllabication, root words, affixes)	256(3, 4); 257(5, 6, 9); 258(11, 12)
5.5—Uses a variety of context clues to decode unknown words (e.g., draws on earlier reading, reads ahead)	87(12); 212(1); 235(7); 256(2); 257(7)
5.7—Understands level-appropriate reading vocabulary (e.g., synonyms, antonyms, homophones, multi-meaning words)	214(11); 215(14); 257(5)
5.8—Monitors own reading strategies and makes modifications as needed (e.g., recognizes when he or she is confused by a section of text, questions whether the text makes sense)	132(7); 214(12); 215(13); 233(3)
5.10—Understands the author's purpose (e.g., to persuade, to inform) or point of view	23(8, 11); 24(14); 42(1, 2); 43(3, 4, 5, 6); 44(7, 8, 9, 10, 11); 173(8); 190(3, 4)

Correlation to Standards *(cont.)*

Standard/Objective	Page (Strategy)
7.3—Uses text organizers (e.g., headings, topic and summary sentences, graphic features, typeface, chapter titles) to determine the main ideas and to locate information in a text	24(13); 44(11); 64(7); 128(1); 129(2, 3); 130(4); 131(5); 132(7); 133(8); 171(1, 2, 3, 4); 173(6, 7, 8, 9, 10); 174(11, 12, 13, 14); 192(14)
7.4—Uses the various parts of a book (e.g., index, table of contents, glossary, appendix, preface) to locate information	189(1, 2); 190(3, 4, 5); 191(6, 7, 8, 9, 10, 11); 192(12, 13, 14, 15)
7.5—Summarizes and paraphrases information in texts (e.g., includes the main idea and significant supporting details of a reading selection)	66(11); 88(13, 14); 112(15, 16); 129(2, 3); 130(4); 131(5); 132(6, 7); 133(8); 150(1); 174(12); 213(4, 5, 6); 232(1); 233(2, 3); 234(4, 5, 6); 235(7); 236(9, 10); 257(8)
7.6—Uses prior knowledge and experience to understand and respond to new information	23(12); 63(2, 3); 64(5, 7); 65(8, 9, 10); 66(11, 12, 13); 86(6, 7); 87(8, 9, 10, 11); 110(5, 6); 111(10); 112(13, 14); 129(2, 3); 132(6); 154(5); 189(2); 190(4); 213(5, 6, 8); 214(9, 10); 215(15); 216(19); 234(5, 6); 236(8); 256(2, 3); 257(10)
7.7—Understands structural patterns or organization in informational texts (e.g., chronological, logical, or sequential order; compare and contrast; cause and effect; proposition and support)	132(7); 134(9); 150(1); 151(2); 152(3); 153(4); 154(5); 155(6, 7, 8); 172(5); 213(7)
8.2—Asks questions in class (e.g., when he or she is confused, to seek others' opinions and comments)	22(4, 5); 64(6, 7); 85(1, 2); 86(3, 4, 5); 87(9); 108(1); 109(2, 3, 4); 110(5, 7, 8); 111(9, 10, 11); 112(13, 14, 16); 173(9, 10); 190(4); 192(13)
8.15—Knows specific ways in which language is used in real-life situations (e.g., buying something from a shopkeeper, requesting something from a parent, arguing with a sibling, talking to a friend)	155(6); 257(10)
8.16—Understands that language reflects different regions and cultures (e.g., sayings; expressions; usage; oral traditions and customs; historical, geographical, and societal influences on language)	216(18); 235(7); 257(9)

PASSPORT TO COMPREHENSION

Monitor
Comprehension

Monitor Comprehension—
Set the Purpose

Introduction

All meaningful reading needs a purpose. Even without explicitly or consciously stating why they are reading, strategic readers survey the reading material and assess why they are reading it. This technique helps to establish how to read a particular piece of writing. The traditional setting for teachers to provide students with a purpose for reading is when giving an assignment. Although helpful to some students, this method does not allow students to determine their own purposes for reading. Consequently, less proficient readers wait until the purpose is set for them and then read only to obtain that small piece of specified information. Very little actual learning takes place in this setting.

Activities before and during reading require students to be actively involved in the process. Effective strategies are those that ask students to monitor their own comprehension and progress. Referred to as *metacomprehension* (Langer 1987), this self-monitoring system is comprised of two different aspects. First, the student is aware of the goal of the reading assignment and has determined what is already known about the topic, what needs to be learned, and which strategies are necessary to gain comprehension. Second, the student engages in regulatory activities that arise as a result of self-monitoring. Another way of putting it is, what does the reader do when things go wrong? Teachers need to be aware that telling students merely to "read carefully" or "look up the information" is not effective when students don't even realize that something has "gone wrong" in their reading. The ultimate goal of these strategies is for students to realize intrinsic or internalized purposes from their reading, thus achieving greater interaction with the text and enhanced comprehension and learning.

The process of reading should begin before a book is opened. Teachers help students become effective, systematic readers by teaching and reinforcing strategies that can be employed before, during, and after reading. Direct instruction of strategies is essential and should be accompanied by relevant explanations of why the strategies are helpful in learning, by instruction in when these strategies are used, and by extensive modeling of the strategies in appropriate reading contexts. Relevant explanations are important in motivating students to use the reading strategies. Direct instruction and modeling are important because inappropriately or incorrectly applied strategies can hinder rather than help reading and can discourage students from using similar strategies in the future.

Effective readers are those who identify a purpose for reading and select appropriate strategies to meet the reading goal for a particular passage. These strategies include those that activate prior knowledge and provide anticipation for what they will read or hear. They also direct students' attention to the major points in the reading, point out how a text is organized, teach unfamiliar vocabulary or concepts, and provide students with a purpose for reading or listening (Irvin 1998). When students are able to state the purpose for reading a particular source, they can effectively choose suitable materials to read, as well as determine appropriate reading strategies to utilize. Specific strategies that are used before and during reading help to set a purpose (establish a goal) for reading. Many of the strategies used for setting a purpose are the same as, or similar to, those used for understanding text organization, analyzing structural patterns, and using the various parts of the book.

Monitor Comprehension— Set the Purpose

Stating the Purpose

Most of the time we give students their purpose for reading. We tell them that they will be reading to learn about a particular topic such as the War of 1812 in social studies, doing long division in math, the French Impressionists in art, or habitats for various creatures in science. Providing students with their purpose for reading is fine, but it is also important to develop instructional strategies in which students are led to a predetermined purpose for reading or to decide for themselves what their purpose will be. Various purposes include reading to:

- be entertained

- be informed

- be persuaded

- learn how to do something

- analyze the author

- reflect upon and extend personal experience and prior knowledge

- generate questions for further research about the topic or concept

- gather information for a discussion

It is important that students keep a purpose in mind while they are reading in order to sort and organize new information, connect it to their purpose for reading, and be able to articulate and justify how the information they have gained helps them achieve the purpose for reading.

Choosing Appropriate Materials to Read

Once students know and understand their purpose for reading, they should be given opportunities to select texts that will help them to achieve their purpose. Students need to be taught how to preview the text, skim for main ideas and supporting details, make note of headings and subheadings, critically analyze graphic features, and read carefully the back cover, inside cover, and any other surface information that will help them to determine the appropriateness of the text.

Using Appropriate Strategies for Different Purposes

Being able to set the purpose for reading is a vital first step toward developing strategic reading skills. Students need to be able to skim and scan effectively in order to locate information quickly. They need to be able to read carefully in order to gain full comprehension, and read critically in order to analyze or interpret the author's intent. These are just some of the skills that students need to meet the purpose for reading. Make sure to expose students to text coding, double-entry journals, buddy journals, discussion techniques, and graphic organizers in order for them to read for entertainment, information, critical analysis of the author, or whatever their purpose may be.

Monitor Comprehension— Set the Purpose

Using Strategies Independently

Model for students how to set an individualized purpose for reading. Start at the school library by allowing students to browse for books at least once every three weeks in order to select a book for enjoyment. Once students have selected books, have them share with the class what they chose and why. Make sure to allow students to choose fiction and nonfiction. As students share, they will see that some classmates chose fiction in the genres of mystery, science fiction, or realistic fiction. They will see that other classmates chose nonfiction about planes, aliens, race cars, or animals. Students will learn that we each read for our own purposes. Expose students to a variety of techniques for book selection: examining the book jacket, reading the inside cover, reading about the author, scanning the chapter titles, reading the first few paragraphs, etc. Make book selection a celebration of independent choice.

Strategy 1: Achieving a Purpose for Reading

Allow students to select a book of their choice and have them identify many purposes for reading. For example, if the student selected a book about horses, he or she might identify the following purposes for reading: to learn about what horses like to eat, to learn about how horses socialize, to learn about the life span of horses, to learn about horse racing and competition, etc. Have students complete the graphic organizer, Achieving a Purpose for Reading (page 25), by recording their purposes, identifying whether or not they achieved their purposes, and writing a brief explanation. (Standard 5.2)

Strategy 2: Text Coding for Purpose

A simple coding strategy that will help students read to achieve their purpose is identified on the Text Coding for Purpose activity on page 26. As students are reading, they mark text with a "P!" for strong connection to purpose and a "P" for some connection to purpose. (If students are not allowed to write directly on the text, have them use sticky notes.) When students finish reading the nonfiction text, have them record the text information that corresponds with the code that they have chosen in the left column of the chart, and then have them write a reaction to the selected text in the right column. Have students reflect on how the information connects to their purpose for reading and their prior knowledge of the subject. (Standard 5.2)

Strategy 3: Previewing a Text for Information

If a students are going to pick and choose areas of a text to read, they still need to be able to state the purpose for reading. If the teacher has given the students questions to answer or an assignment to complete, they should read through all of the questions or the assignment and write their purpose for reading. Students should use the parts of the book and the text organizers to predict where they think the information will be found. Then students can overview or read the sections of text for the information needed. The Previewing a Text for Information guide is on page 27 for practice with this strategy. (Standard 5.2)

Monitor Comprehension— Set the Purpose

Strategy 4: Question/Answer

Begin by having students identify their purpose for reading. Then, lead students in generating a list of prereading questions that will help them to achieve their purpose. For example, if students are reading about the history of baseball and their purpose is to understand the history and know why it's important to the sport today, they may generate several questions such as the following: Who invented the game of baseball? Where was it invented? What were the initial reactions to the game? How do people react to the game today? Students should write their questions in the left column of the Question/Answer chart (page 28) and record the answers as they find them in the text in the right column. Remind students that in order to answer some of the questions, they may need to make some inferences. When students have finished their charts, have them reflect on how the process of questioning helped them to achieve their purpose for reading. (Standards 5.2, 8.2)

Strategy 5: Question/Answer/Reaction

Using the activity on page 29, follow the same procedures as the Question/Answer strategy. However, this time have students write brief reactions to the answers that they found. (Standards 5.2, 8.2) Some helpful sentence starters include:

> I was surprised to learn that…
>
> This information confirms what I knew about…
>
> I agree/disagree because…

Strategy 6: Examining Multiple Texts

A great way to motivate students to examine multiple texts is to present them with a purpose for reading and then take them to the school library and have them select books to achieve their purpose. For example, imagine that their purpose for reading is to learn about the solar system. Students could go to the library and find books that explain the facts of each planet, the history of space travel, the mythology of the constellations, or information about comets, asteroids, and meteors. Have them use the Examining Multiple Texts activity on page 30 to preview three different texts and to think about how the texts would help them to achieve their purpose for reading. Instruct students to select the best text and read more deeply to acquire the necessary information. (Standards 5.1, 5.2)

Strategy 7: Reading the Entire Text

Even if students are going to read the entire nonfiction text, they still need to employ prereading strategies. Readers need to state their purpose for reading. If the teacher has given students a set of questions about the text or a writing assignment on the topic, they can read through the questions or the assignment and then write a statement as to the purpose for reading the text. The written statement should encompass all of the teacher's questions and show that students understand why they are reading the text. After students have stated their purpose for reading, they can use all of the skills mentioned throughout this book. The Reading the Entire Text activity is on page 31. (Standard 5.2)

Monitor Comprehension— Set the Purpose

Strategy 8: Author and Me Analysis

It is important for students to understand that they read for a variety of purposes, but that authors also write for a variety of purposes. Use the activity on page 32 to have students identify their purpose and the author's purpose. Chances are, if students are reading to be informed, the author was also writing to inform. As students are reading, they record important information in the left column and make connections to their purpose for reading and the author's purpose for writing in the remaining columns. (Standards 5.2, 5.10)

Strategy 9: Reading to Be Entertained

Students should know that text contains information that is highly interesting and motivating. Expose students to interesting, engaging text as often as possible. Have them use the activity on page 33 to record interesting, funny, or entertaining text in the left column and a reaction to the text in the right column. To foster the message that reading is fun, make sure to have a large collection of nonfiction materials available to students and to frequently read aloud to students in a way that is engaging and entertaining. (Standard 5.2)

Strategy 10: Reading to Be Informed

In content-area classrooms, one of the most common purposes for reading is to be informed. Create an atmosphere where learning is valuable and informational text is viewed as intriguing. Distribute the activity on page 34. Have students record facts and details in the left column, and write a reaction in the right column. Make sure students think about why the author wanted them to learn the information, why the information will be valuable to them, and any further questions they may have. (Standard 5.2)

Strategy 11: Reading to Be Persuaded

We are surrounded by text that is intended to be persuasive. Have students read a variety of texts that are persuasive and show them how to analyze the author's use of rhetorical language, examples, and appeals to the audience in order to make his or her argument convincing. Distribute the activity on page 35 and have students record text information that is persuasive. In the right column, have the students write a reaction to the choices that the author made and why those choices made the text convincing. Allow students to identify ideas with which they disagree or text that is not convincing. (Standard 5.10)

Strategy 12: Reading to Extend Prior Knowledge

Extending and enriching students' prior knowledge about a subject can be very beneficial in deepening their understanding. As an introductory activity to reading information on a topic that is already familiar to students, have them sit in a circle, and in round-robin fashion, share something they know about the topic or concept. As a variation, begin with a KWL chart to have them identify their prior knowledge. Distribute the activity on page 36 and have students record information in the left column that connects to what they already know as they are reading. (Standard 7.6)

Monitor Comprehension— Set the Purpose

Strategy 13: Using the Phone Directory

Have you ever tried to find a phone number in the yellow pages and not known under what topic to look? Bring in a few old yellow page phone directories so that students can become familiar with them. Explain that the numbers of stores and businesses are listed under the types of stores or businesses they are. Sometimes a store can be listed under more than one heading because it serves many purposes. Find a few stores with which the students would be familiar. Brainstorm under what heading information about the store or business would be found in the phone directory. For instance:

The Haircut Place

Barber

Hairstyling

Hair

Beauty

Try looking up a few of these stores and businesses. Explain to students that in the same way, they can find information on their topic under many different headings. They need to brainstorm related ideas in order to find all appropriate reading material. Use the activity on page 37 to practice this strategy. (Standard 7.3)

Strategy 14: Analyzing the Author's Purpose

For this activity, students will analyze the author. Students will record text information that reveals the author's purpose for writing on the left side of the chart and then react to the information on the right side of the chart. Use the activity on page 38. (Standard 5.10)

Strategy 15: Purpose and Learning "How to"

Students will encounter sets of instructions, recipes, and rule books their entire lives and will need to know how to read critically in order to create a product or learn the necessary information to know how to do something. Have students identify something that they would like to learn how to do or to make. Take them to the school library and allow them to find resources that fit their learning objectives. Distribute the Purpose and Learning "How to" activity on page 39, and have students record the step-by-step instructions in the left column in paraphrased form. Have them write a reaction by analyzing whether or not the instructions were clear, determining the effectiveness of the graphic features, and identifying any further questions they have based on areas of confusion. As an extension, students can identify something that they know how to do quite well. Allow students to choose simple skills, such as making a peanut butter and jelly sandwich, cleaning their rooms, or catching a fly ball to the outfield. Instruct students to write a set of instructions, switch with a classmate, and analyze each other's writing for clarity of thought as well as appropriate graphic features that would enhance the text. You could also do this extension as a whole-class activity. The class could help you write a set of instructions, and then you can act out the instructions as they are written to make sure you remembered each step and the necessary details. (Standard 5.2)

Monitor Comprehension—
Set the Purpose

Achieving a Purpose for Reading

Directions: Use this chart to identify your purposes for reading. Be very specific. For example, if your purpose is to be informed, identify specifically the information about which you would like to be informed. After reading, determine whether or not you achieved your purpose and write an explanation.

What are my purposes for reading?	Did I achieve my purpose?		Explanation
	YES	NO	
	YES	NO	
	YES	NO	
	YES	NO	
	YES	NO	
	YES	NO	

Monitor Comprehension— Set the Purpose

Text Coding for Purpose

Directions: Before reading, identify your purpose. As you are reading, mark the text using the following codes. Then, record the text that corresponds with the codes in the left column. Write a reaction using the guiding questions in the right column.

P! = Strong Connection to Purpose for Reading

P = Some Connection to Purpose for Reading

Purpose for Reading: _____

_____

Text information that connects to my purpose for reading	Reaction: How does this information connect to my purpose for reading? How does this information connect to my prior knowledge of the subject? What further questions do I have?

Monitor Comprehension— Set the Purpose

Previewing a Text for Information

Title: _____

1. Read the questions or the assignment your teacher has given you. Write a short statement of what you think the purpose of reading this text is.

   _____

   _____

   _____

2. Use key words to determine the text structure (compare and contrast, cause and effect, proposition and support, progression of ideas).

   _____

   _____

   _____

3. Using the text organizers, predict in what section or sections of the text you will find the information you need.

   _____

   _____

   _____

4. Now read or preview the sections where you predicted your information would be found. Were your predictions correct?

   _____

Monitor Comprehension—
Set the Purpose

Question/Answer

Directions: Before reading, record questions that will help you to achieve your purpose for reading. As you read, record the answers to the questions.

My purpose for reading: _____

My questions about the text information	Answers

How did questioning help me to achieve my purpose for reading? _____

_____

_____

_____

Monitor Comprehension—
Set the Purpose

Question/Answer/Reaction

Directions: Before reading, use this chart to record questions that will help you to achieve your purpose for reading. Record the answers as you read. After reading, write a reaction to the text information you found.

My purpose for reading: _____

_____

My questions	Answers	Reactions

Monitor Comprehension—
Set the Purpose

Examining Multiple Texts

Directions: Establish your purpose for reading. Look through three different texts. Compare each text and determine how each text will help you achieve your purpose for reading.

Purpose for Reading: _____

Text #1: _____

Information gained through previewing (topics, concepts, ideas): _____

_____

_____

_____

How will this text help me to achieve my purpose for reading? _____

_____

_____

Text #2: _____

Information gained through previewing (topics, concepts, ideas): _____

_____

_____

How will this text help me to achieve my purpose for reading? _____

_____

_____

Text #3: _____

Information gained through previewing (topics, concepts, ideas): _____

_____

_____

_____

How will this text help me to achieve my purpose for reading? _____

_____

_____

Monitor Comprehension— Set the Purpose

Reading the Entire Text

Title: _____

1. Read the questions or the assignment your teacher has given you. Write a short statement of what you think the purpose for reading this text is.

    _____

    _____

2. Use key words to determine the text structure (compare and contrast, cause and effect, proposition and support, progression of ideas).

    _____

    _____

3. Create a graphic organizer (KWL chart or idea web using the chapters listed in the table of contents or using the text organizers, etc.) to organize your thoughts about the book.

4. Now read your text while focusing on the information you wish to find.

Monitor Comprehension— Set the Purpose

Author and Me Analysis

Directions: Use the following chart to compare your purpose for reading with the author's purpose for writing.

My purpose for reading: _____

_____

The author's purpose for writing: _____

_____

Important information	How does this information connect to the author's purpose for writing?	How does this information connect to my purpose for reading?

Monitor Comprehension—
Set the Purpose

Reading to Be Entertained

Directions: Your purpose for reading is to be entertained. As you read, record text information that is interesting, funny, or entertaining on the left side of the chart and then react to the information on the right side of the chart.

Title of the text: _____

Text that is interesting, funny, or entertaining	Reaction: How does the text make me feel? How does the information relate to my life? Why is the text interesting or funny?

Monitor Comprehension— Set the Purpose

Reading to Be Informed

Directions: Your purpose for reading is to be informed. As you read, record text information that is informative, factual, or helps you to learn about the topic or concept. Record text information that is informative on the left side of the chart and then react to the information on the right side of the chart.

Title of the text: _____

Text information that helps me to learn about the topic or concept	Reaction: What was the most important information I learned? What were the most important facts or details I learned? Why? What did the author want me to learn from this information? Do I have any further questions?

Monitor Comprehension— Set the Purpose

Reading to Be Persuaded

Directions: Your purpose for reading is to be persuaded about the topic. As you read, record text information that is convincing and persuasive on the left side of the chart and then react to the information on the right side of the chart.

Title of the text: _____

Text information that is convincing or persuasive (Remember to examine carefully the content of the text and the graphic features.)	Reaction: Why is this information persuasive? Does the author use language, examples, or graphic features that are particularly convincing? Explain. Will I take action as a result of this information? How could the information be more persuasive?

Is there any part of the text that you don't agree with or that is not convincing? Explain.

_____

_____

Monitor Comprehension—
Set the Purpose

Reading to Extend Prior Knowledge

Directions: Your purpose for reading is to extend your prior knowledge. As you read, record text information that connects to what you already know about the topic or concept on the left side of the chart and then react to the information on the right side of the chart.

Title of the text: _____

Text information that connects to your personal experience or prior knowledge of the topic or concept	Reaction: How does this information connect to my personal experience or prior knowledge? Does this information surprise me or confirm what I already know? Do I agree or disagree with any of the information? Explain.

Monitor Comprehension—
Set the Purpose

Using the Phone Directory

Directions: At the top of each column, write down the five businesses that your teacher has chosen. Brainstorm at least four headings under which you might find each business. Write those under the name of the business.

Example: **The Haircut Place**

Barber

Hair

Hairstyling

Beauty

Look up the headings you brainstormed. Under which headings did you find each business? On the lines below, write (in a complete sentence) where you found each business.

Example: The Haircut Place can be found under the headings of Barber and Hairstyling.

_____

_____

_____

_____

_____

Monitor Comprehension—
Set the Purpose

Analyzing the Author's Purpose

Directions: Your purpose for reading is to analyze the author. As you read, record text information that reveals the author's purpose on the left side of the chart and then react to the information on the right side of the chart.

Title of the text: _____

Text information that reveals the author's purpose	Reaction: What does the author want me to learn about the topic? What language choices does the author use to achieve his/her purpose? What graphic features does the author include to achieve his/her purpose? How do the author's examples achieve his/her purpose?

Monitor Comprehension—
Set the Purpose

Purpose and Learning "How to"

Directions: Your purpose for reading is to learn how to do something. As you read, record text information that teaches you how to achieve your task on the left side of the chart and then react to the information on the right side of the chart.

Title of the text: _____

Text information that teaches how to do something	Reaction: Are the instructions clear? How could the instructions be more clear? How could the author have included more graphic features to clarify the instructions? What questions do I still have? Based on what I've learned, could I teach someone else how to achieve the task?

Monitor Comprehension—Author's Point of View

Introduction

Being able to analyze an author's viewpoint is a critical reading skill, essential for building the deepest levels of understanding textual information. Building a mental picture of the author is challenging for young children to do; therefore, students will need extensive teacher modeling. When young readers are able to understand the author's viewpoint, they will be able to evaluate the author's word choice, style, and language structure. Ultimately, students will think of themselves as authors and apply their critical skills to their own writing in order to meet the needs of their intended audience.

Differentiating Between Fact and Opinion

Authors write for many purposes: to inform, to persuade, to express personal ideas, to teach, and to entertain. When they choose their examples and supporting details in informational and persuasive writing, authors use a blend of facts and opinions. It is important for readers to be able to distinguish between facts and opinions so that they can sort text. The text should be sorted into information that they should retain about the topic and information that is the viewpoint of the author, which is essential for evaluating the integrity of the author, but not necessarily critical to remember. Readers should know that authors sometimes attempt to disguise opinions as facts in order to strengthen their case. Critical readers will be able to recognize when they are being manipulated and think about the text in terms of the credibility of the author.

Understanding the Author's Word Choice

When presenting informational text, authors should use calm, precise, controlled language. The words in the text should reflect a rational author, knowledgeable about the topic and intent on informing or teaching the reader about the topic. This stance does not mean that the text should be dry and uninteresting. Good informational writers use rhetorical questions, incorporate figurative language when appropriate, and vary their sentence length and structure. Most authors not only want the information to be accessible but also want to achieve their purpose by allowing the reader to "enter" into the text comfortably by making the word choice and language interesting, compelling, and appropriate to the audience's knowledge level, age, and experiences.

Understanding the Author's Use of Language Structure

When authors use a variety of sentence lengths and structures, the information is more interesting to the reader because the ideas flow smoothly. In addition, information should be presented in an organizational structure that is appropriate to the author's purpose. Authors use description, cause-effect, compare-contrast, problem-solution, proposition-support, and sequence to present information. Organizational structure provides a framework for readers to learn the information, and proficient readers will recognize the structure that the author is using and anticipate how the information will unfold. When authors appropriately use language structure, they build their credibility in the reader's mind. Readers assume that if the author is skilled at presenting the information, he or she is also knowledgeable about the topic.

Monitor Comprehension— Author's Point of View

Using Context to Determine the Author's Viewpoint

It is important for readers to understand that there is a context in which the author's viewpoint is created. Questions that will help determine the context include:

1. What is the setting connected to the information? (time and place)

2. Identify the time and place in which the author lives.

3. What are other events connected to the topic?

4. Identify other people who are connected to the topic.

5. What is the author's connection to the topic?

Sometimes context is irrelevant or difficult to determine. When working with many different kinds of text, it may be difficult to get information about the author and his or her connection to the topic. However, when accessible and appropriate, teachers can provide students with such information about the author and any other outside information relevant to the topic. Understanding context will help students become critical, analytical readers.

Understanding Techniques Used to Convey Viewpoint

There are many techniques that authors use to convey their views on a topic. Authors may include personal experience stories, carefully chosen facts and statistics, as well as expert opinions from various sources. Once again, critical readers need to know when such techniques are being used so that they can determine whether or not the information they are reading is biased or fairly presented.

Evaluating and Extending the Author's Meaning

All of the techniques and strategies presented in this section are intended to guide teachers in helping students evaluate and extend the author's meaning. The following questions may also help students evaluate the author:

- How did the author introduce the topic? Was this approach effective?
- How did the author use language to make the topic interesting?
- What information should the author have added?
- What information could the author delete?
- What questions do you have for the author?
- What new questions do you have about the topic?

Using Strategies Independently

Evaluating the author is a challenging task. Begin teaching this skill by crafting some original writing about a topic and sharing your writing with students. Allow them to ask questions of you, an author, face-to-face. Allow them to critique you and give suggestions regarding things you should add or delete. This process will help students to visualize authors as real people.

Monitor Comprehension— Author's Point of View

Strategy 1: First-, Second-, and Third-Person Point of View

Much of nonfiction writing is impersonal and, therefore, written in the third-person point of view. This point of view is the most objective, the one that best conveys facts without the intrusion of the author's thoughts, feelings, and opinions. But two other points of view—first and second person—are used in different texts and for different purposes in nonfiction. For example:

- First person: editorials, essays, autobiographies, original source material (diaries, letters, etc.), reviews, eyewitness accounts, text that conveys immediacy

- Second person: advertising, campaign propaganda, brochures, text with which the author wants the reader to identify

- Third person: descriptions, chronologies, research, reports, news items, in-depth articles

Make a habit of asking students to notice this basic point of view whenever they begin to read a new piece of nonfiction. Ask them why the author may have chosen this point of view and how the piece would be changed if it were written from a different point of view. Use the activity on page 45 to practice this strategy. (Standard 5.10)

Strategy 2: Fact vs. Opinion

Somehow students seem to pick up the myth that nonfiction is "true." Thus, it is critical to instruct students in the fact that much of nonfiction has to do with opinion—the author's own beliefs. The following types of nonfiction often contain as much opinion as fact, if not more so:

- reviews of products, films, music, restaurants
- social studies texts that reflect bias toward gender, race, or political stance
- magazine articles on controversial current events
- biographies that reflect an author's admiration for his or her subject

Begin by presenting students with pairs of sentences, one reflecting fact and one reflecting opinion, like those shown below. You also may use the Fact vs. Opinion activity on page 46 to initiate your discussion. Thereafter, use sentence pairs that relate to a text you currently are reading in class.

> **Fact:** Roses need specific amounts of nitrogen, water, and sun to produce large blooms.
>
> **Opinion:** All roses are most lovely when they are in full bloom.
>
> **Fact:** School cafeteria food includes a variety of items from the five food groups.
>
> **Opinion:** When meat is included in the school cafeteria menu, it is no longer nutritious.

Point out to students that facts are difficult to dispute. Roses do have very specific requirements; they cannot grow in the shade, for example. Opinions, on the other hand, can be debated (e.g., people may find roses beautiful at different stages of their growth, not necessarily just when they're in full bloom). In the second pair of sentences, the first one comes from well-accepted research; the second comes from what appears to be a vegetarian author who does not see the value of meat as part of the school menu. Opinions provoke debate; without support, they do not hold up to examination in the way that facts do. Facts can be disputed as well, but usually it requires some investigation. An opinion can be changed in the snap of the fingers. Use the activities on pages 46 and 47 to help students differentiate between fact and opinion. (Standard 5.10)

Monitor Comprehension— Author's Point of View

Strategy 3: Fact/Opinion Partner Chart

Have students read text that contains a blend of facts and opinions. Then give them a chart with three categories: facts, the author's opinion of the topic, and my opinion of the topic. Have students complete the chart and then discuss the differences between fact and opinion. Also have them discuss the similarities and differences between their opinions and the author's opinions. As a variation, have students work with a partner and use the Fact/Opinion Partner Chart on page 48 to record facts from the text and the opinions of each partner. Make sure to emphasize that authors use a blend of facts and opinions intentionally to achieve their purpose. Awareness of what authors do will help student authors be critical readers, as well as apply these techniques to their own writing. (Standard 5.10)

Strategy 4: Evaluating the Author's Word Choice

Students read examples of text on page 49 and identify whether or not the examples are specific and controlled or biased and overly emotional. Then students record specific instances of the author's word choice and again determine how the words were used. (Standard 5.10)

Strategy 5: Avoiding Bias in Storytelling

Have students sit in a large circle. Begin by telling two simple stories about your morning. The first story should include language that is calm, reasonable, and non-biased. Present the facts only. The second story should involve the same information but should include overly emotional, biased judgments about the events of your morning. The following example might be helpful:

Story 1: This morning I woke up to the sound of my alarm clock. I fed my cat and made some breakfast for my family. Then I jumped in the shower. I got dressed and brushed my teeth. I said goodbye to my family and got in my car. It was raining outside so I drove very carefully! I got to school and came to our classroom to get ready for the day.

Story 2: Waking up to the annoying sound of my alarm clock this morning was the worst way to start my day! I had to feed my cat right away or else he would follow me around all morning. I started to make breakfast for everyone in my family, but I had to rush around and I accidentally burned the toast. I rushed out the door so I wouldn't be late and I almost forgot my keys! I learned that it was raining outside and I was so upset because I hate the rain! Every other car was driving like crazy. I arrived at school and rushed to our classroom before the bell rang. It was a very hectic morning.

Then, give students a topic such as "our major league football team" or "lunchtime in our school." Students go around the circle, and each tells one non-biased sentence about the topic. Then, they go around again and tell one sentence that is overly emotional and judgmental. Discuss with students how important it is for them to use reasonable, rational language and examples when presenting information in order to prove their credibility as writers. As a follow-up to this activity, use the activity on page 50 titled Avoiding Bias in Storytelling for students to determine propaganda techniques. (Standard 5.10)

Strategy 6: Thinking About the Author's Point of View

After you have completed several of these activities, give students a chance to show their understanding of the concept of author's viewpoint by having them complete page 51. (Standard 5.10)

Monitor Comprehension— Author's Point of View

Strategy 7: Using Context to Determine the Author's Viewpoint

When possible, share information about the author with students. Have them go to the school library to research information about the author and create a mini-biography. Discuss how the author's life affects his or her ideas and viewpoints that students found in the text. They can also create a "mock" biography and make inferences about the author's life based on the way he or she presents information, his or her knowledge base, and his or her viewpoint on the topic. Use the activity on page 52. (Standard 5.10)

Strategy 8: Listening for and Evaluating the Author's Voice

Arrange students in a large circle and have them take turns reading the same piece of text. This time they are listening for the author's voice. When students have finished reading, have them generate a list of words to describe the voice of the writer and examples from the text to back up their opinions. You may want to make a transparency of Listening for and Evaluating the Author's Voice (page 53) and record students' observations on the overhead. As a variation, have students read the text in round-robin fashion a second time and intentionally try to give the author a different voice by using a different tone in their reading. Discuss whether this different voice matches the author's purpose. (Standard 5.10)

Strategy 9: Creating a Balanced Opinion

In this strategy, the teacher will take on the role of the author. Divide the class in half. One half of the class works with a partner to prove that you (the author) presented your ideas in a balanced manner. Students will have to find specific examples from the text to prove their point and generate questions that will help you show that you presented the information fairly. The other half of the class will work with a partner to prove that you (the author) did not present your ideas in a balanced manner. These students will also find examples from the text and generate questions. After students have prepared for the trial, you will sit in the middle of the two sides. Each side will choose a spokesperson to ask questions and try to prove their point about your ability to present the information in a balanced manner. This strategy works especially well with proposition and support texts. For example, if your students are reading about ways to improve schools, the text may present a variety of ideas and propositions. One side might claim that you (the author) gave good ideas that help schools in many ways. However, the other side might claim that you (the author) left out many other good ideas or that your ideas will only help certain schools. Use the activity on page 54 to practice this strategy. (Standard 5.10)

Strategy 10: Visualizing and Analyzing the Intended Audience

While you are trying to get students to visualize the author and understand his or her purpose and choices, it is also important that students realize that effective authors will visualize and analyze the audience in order to appeal to their needs, beliefs, and interests. Use the activity on pages 55 and 56 to guide students in visualizing and analyzing the audience the author was trying to reach. (Standard 5.10)

Strategy 11: Double-Entry Journal

Double-entry journals are a great way for students to select significant text information and think critically about the information. Having students evaluate the author's organization and/or purpose using a double-entry journal format is a highly effective technique (see pages 57 and 58). (Standards 5.10, 7.3)

Monitor Comprehension— Author's Point of View

First-, Second-, and Third-Person Point of View

Like fiction, nonfiction can be written from three different points of view. Which one is used will depend on the type of writing and the author's purpose.

First-person point of view:

- "I" is the narrator
- Subjective writing that includes opinions and feelings
- Eyewitness accounts, editorials, autobiographies, essays, reviews
- Example: I remember the Northridge earthquake well.

Second-person point of view:

- Refers to "you" in the narrative
- Writing that the author wants the reader to identify with
- Advertising, propaganda, campaign messages
- Example: Your vote is needed to put a stop to ocean pollution.

Third-person point of view:

- Objective writing that omits opinions and feelings
- News items, in-depth articles, reports, research, history and science texts, how-to manuals
- Example: To assemble, insert Tab A into Slot B and give one-quarter turn.

Directions: Complete the following activities.

1. Rewrite the following in the third-person point of view, as if you were writing an objective report. Share your paragraph with classmates.

   As the flood waters rose, I began to grab belongings and haul them out to the car. I heard a tree branch snap in the wind, then fall to the ground with a thunderous crunch. My neighbor's windshield was demolished! I jumped into my own car and sped away. Water completely covered the bridge. I turned around, knowing that my only hope was to go further inland where, hopefully, the rain hadn't fallen so hard.

2. Find a paragraph in a news item and rewrite it in the first-person point of view. Be creative and add interesting details such as your own thoughts and feelings. Share your paragraph with classmates.

3. Write an advertisement for a popular soft drink in the second-person point of view. Try to get your reader motivated to buy the product by identifying with what you write. Share your ad with your classmates.

Monitor Comprehension— Author's Point of View

Fact vs. Opinion

Directions: Many types of nonfiction contain opinions as well as facts. Opinions are statements that can be debated because they are based on information that cannot be proven. Facts are statements that can be proven and are not easily argued. To change a factual statement, there may even need to be experimentation or investigation. Read the statements below and determine which is an opinion and which is a fact.

Peppermint makes a refreshing iced tea.

Peppermint can be used to help settle an upset stomach.

The first statement is an opinion. The statement can be debated because people who dislike peppermint may not find it to be refreshing. The second statement is a fact. Mint has been used in many cultures to help ease the stomach. Also, the second statement uses conditional language. It says that peppermint *can* be used; it does not say peppermint *must* be used.

Often, opinions make broad generalizations while facts are very specific. Read the statements below to determine which is broad and which is specific.

For many young people, listening to loud music helps them release tension.

Everyone loves to relax by dancing and listening to music.

The second statement, an opinion, is broad. Look at the language of the sentence. The word "everyone" means just that. Is this statement true? Does everyone love to relax by listening to music? The first statement, a fact, is specific. It contains specific adjectives: "many," "young," "loud." If you investigated the statement, you would most likely find that it is true, or mostly so.

Directions: Read the statements below. Place an **O** by the ones that are opinions and an **F** by facts.

1. No one likes to go to the beach when it is cold. _____

2. Many people save money at the market by clipping coupons. _____

3. Cats are always annoying. _____

4. Green is a restful color for a bedroom. _____

5. Hummingbirds move very quickly as they travel from flower to flower. _____

6. The best way to cook a potato is by boiling. _____

7. To keep gardens free of weeds, use plenty of mulch such as wood chips. _____

8. All toddlers love to chew on plain bagels. _____

9. Many people give one another flowers on Valentine's Day. _____

10. The best cake for a party is chocolate. _____

Monitor Comprehension— Author's Point of View

Differentiating Between Fact and Opinion

Directions: Use this activity page to evaluate the author's use of fact and opinion in the text.

Remember: A fact is something that can be proven. An opinion conveys thoughts, feelings, or ideas that cannot be proven.

1. Topic: _____

2. Intended audience: _____

3. Author's purpose: _____

   _____

4. Author's thesis: _____

   _____

5. Facts included: _____

   _____

   _____

6. Opinions included: _____

   _____

   _____

7. Does the author use mostly facts, mostly opinions, or a balance of both? How do you know? _____

   _____

   _____

8. Does the author achieve his or her purpose? Why or why not? Support your opinion with examples from the text. _____

   _____

   _____

Monitor Comprehension—
Author's Point of View

Fact/Opinion Partner Chart

Directions: With your partner, read the assigned text selection. Find as many facts as you can on your topic and come up with opinions on the topic.

Topic: _____

Facts from text	Opinions of partner 1	Opinions of partner 2

Monitor Comprehension—
Author's Point of View

Evaluating the Author's Word Choice

Part I

Directions: Read the examples of text below and identify whether or not the examples are specific and controlled or biased and overly emotional. Use a "smiley face" to identify precise, controlled language and a "sad face" to identify biased, highly emotional language.

Remember: Persuasive and informational language

- is calm and reasonable
- includes reasons and specific examples
- avoids exaggerations, words that show strong emotions, bias, anger, and insults

1. During the American Revolution, the British troops repeatedly attempted to conquer the colonists, but to no avail. Patriots such as Patrick Henry, Thomas Jefferson, George Washington, and Thomas Paine served to champion the cause of democracy and remind the colonists of their ultimate goal: freedom.

   Draw a smiley face or a sad face here:_____

2. The British troops during the American Revolution were so stupid! They killed the colonists just because they felt like it. If they had gotten their act together, they might have won. Good thing the colonists stuck together.

   Draw a smiley face or a sad face here:_____

Part II

Directions: Read the above text carefully. Record, in the left-hand column, specific sentences that illustrate the author's word choice. Then draw a smiley face to indicate precise word choice or a sad face to indicate biased or overly emotional word choice in the right-hand column.

Examples of the author's word choice from the text	Evaluation of the author's word choice

Monitor Comprehension—Author's Point of View

Avoiding Bias in Storytelling

Directions: Read the propaganda techniques listed in Part I. Label each of the sentences in Part II with the correct propaganda technique.

Part I

➤ **Testimonial**—Persuasive statements made by people who claim to have personal experience with the issue

➤ **Bandwagon**—Statements intended to make the reader believe that "everyone is doing or believing" what the author is writing about

➤ **Name-calling**—Represents any alternative viewpoints negatively

➤ **Facts left out**—Leaves out facts that may influence the reader toward the author's viewpoint

➤ **Opinions as facts**—Represents the opinions of the author as factual information

➤ **Use of numbers and statistics**—Uses numbers to give the subject greater importance

➤ **Quotation out of context**—Quotes the source of information without providing all the information

➤ **Red herring**—Information intended to mislead the reader

Part II

Sentence or Scenario	Propaganda Technique
"My classmates are a bunch of idiots. They always harass other kids. They are obnoxious bullies!"	
"Ninety-seven percent of all doctors agree that this toothpaste is truly the best for preventing cavities. Ninety-nine percent of customers agree."	
"The necklace is the most beautiful one I've ever seen. It is exquisite and represents the utmost in elegance."	
"Everyone agrees that our vaporizer is the best for helping kids recover from colds. Moms everywhere are buying this vaporizer. Please join moms from around the country and purchase our vaporizer."	
"This hair color product will give you vibrant, luxurious hair." (The advertisement left out the fact that the hair color product causes 5% of women to lose their hair.)	
"The characters in the movie are one-of-a-kind." The following information was omitted from the quotation: "They were rude, fake, and unbelievable!"	
"I can attest to the quality of this product. I have used it for the past thirty years and LOVE it!"	
"This dish detergent will leave your hands soft and smooth." (This ad misled the reader because it failed to mention whether the detergent actually cleans dishes!)	

Monitor Comprehension—
Author's Point of View

Thinking About the Author's Point of View

I wonder why the author _____

_____

_____

_____

I agree with the author about _____

_____

_____

_____

I disagree with the author about _____

_____

_____

_____

I'd like to ask the author _____

_____

_____

_____

The author wants me to remember _____

_____

_____

_____

Monitor Comprehension— Author's Point of View

Using Context to Determine the Author's Viewpoint

Directions: Context is the "big picture" surrounding the topic about which the author is writing. After filling out the chart to identify various aspects of context, answer the question below.

Time and place in which text information is set:	Time and place in which the author lives:
Events connected to the topic:	People connected to the topic:
Author's connection to the topic:	Audience's viewpoint on the topic:

Choose one of the aspects of context listed above. How does this particular aspect affect the author's viewpoint? Explain with as much detail as possible.

_____

_____

_____

_____

_____

_____

_____

_____

_____

_____

Monitor Comprehension— Author's Point of View

Listening for and Evaluating the Author's Voice

Directions: Use the following graphic organizer to analyze the author's voice.

Remember: Voice is the way the author talks about a subject. Voice usually reveals his or her personality, as well as his or her beliefs or feelings about the subject. Words that describe the author's voice in a text include excited, enthusiastic, cynical, skeptical, judgmental, angry, and concerned.

Topic:_____

Intended Audience: _____

Author's Purpose: _____

_____

Words to describe the author's voice	Support from text

Monitor Comprehension—Author's Point of View

Creating a Balanced Opinion

Directions: Read a piece of persuasive text and evaluate whether or not the author has presented a balanced opinion on the topic. Record positive and negative opinions about the topic, infer the author's overall opinion, and evaluate whether or not the author was balanced in his or her writing.

Remember: It is important for authors to present a balanced opinion so that the reader will take their ideas seriously.

Pros or positive opinions about the topic	Cons or negative opinions about the topic

Author's overall opinion of the subject: _____

_____

_____

Did the author present a balanced view? Explain. _____

_____

_____

_____

Monitor Comprehension— Author's Point of View

Visualizing and Analyzing the Intended Audience

Directions: Read the text and complete this activity page guide in order to understand the audience the author was trying to reach. You will have to make inferences using the author's vocabulary, sentence length, examples, and appeals to the audience's interests or belief system. Since you are part of the audience, you can draw on your own life to answer the questions.

Tip: There may be multiple answers for each question.

1. What are the age and gender of the intended audience? _____

   _____

2. What is the highest level of education of the audience? _____

   _____

3. What is the audience's "job"? _____

4. Where does the audience live (city, country or rural area, suburb, house, apartment, etc.)?

   _____

5. What are the audience's interests? _____

   _____

6. What are the audience's beliefs? _____

   _____

   _____

7. What is the audience's greatest priority? _____

   _____

8. What makes the audience cry? _____

   _____

9. What makes the audience laugh? _____

   _____

Monitor Comprehension—Author's Point of View

Visualizing and Analyzing the Intended Audience *(cont.)*

10. What gives the audience hope? _____

_____

11. What are the audience's dreams? _____

_____

_____

12. What does the audience fear most? _____

_____

_____

_____

13. What does the audience do during free time? _____

_____

_____

_____

14. What does the audience already know about the topic? _____

_____

_____

_____

_____

15. What does the audience want to know about the topic? _____

_____

_____

_____

Monitor Comprehension—Author's Point of View

Double-Entry Journal—Evaluating the Author's Organization

Directions: Use this activity page to evaluate the author's organization.

Topic: _____

Intended Audience: _____

Author's Purpose: _____

_____

Order of main idea and supporting details	Evaluation of author's organization
Main idea: Supporting detail #1: Supporting detail #2: Supporting detail #3: Supporting detail #4:	The author did a (good, fair, poor) job organizing the information because… An alternative way to organize the information is…

Monitor Comprehension— Author's Point of View

Double-Entry Journal—Evaluating the Author's Purpose

Directions: Authors write for different purposes. Some of the most common purposes include:

- writing to inform

- writing to persuade

- writing to teach

- writing to express personal ideas

- writing to entertain

In the chart below, record a particular passage from the text on the left-hand side. Then, explain the author's purpose and the author's overall intention on the right-hand side. Evaluate whether or not the author achieved his or her purpose.

Example from text	Response
	The author's purpose is… I know this because… The author (achieved/did not achieve) his/her purpose because…

PASSPORT TO COMPREHENSION

Activate and Connect

#50469 Successful Strategies

Activate and Connect

Introduction

Connections occur when students bridge what they already know with what they are learning. For strong readers, these connections seem to come easily, but for others, activating and applying prior knowledge is a skill that needs to be learned. The research on the benefit of learning this skill is conclusive. When students engage in prereading activities that make them aware of what they do and do not know about a topic, they approach text with purpose and work to construct meaning from their reading experience. This process is how a student's knowledge base grows and expands.

The skill of making connections can be learned in a variety of ways. You can activate students' prior knowledge simply by having them predict and discuss the content of a short article from its title. Brainstorming knowledge about a topic is another easily learned skill, especially concerning a topic with which students have a good deal of exposure. When students have little exposure to a topic, more involved prereading activities are called for, such as creating a classroom-sized rain forest or taking a field trip before commencing a unit of study.

Whether simple or complex, these prereading activities require that students tap into deeply held cognitive structures called *schemata*. Schemata (*schema* is singular) are the concepts that we develop about people, places, experiences, and events. The metaphors most frequently used to describe a schema are file folders and envelopes, but schemata are more organic in nature. Think of a seed of knowledge, growing and developing over time. For example, a small child knows only the name of a single four-legged animal, "dog." Until he or she has more exposure and cognitive capacity, every four-legged animal is a dog. As the child acquires knowledge, the schema of four-legged animal expands to include cats, squirrels, and rabbits. In other words, the child assimilates or adds to the schema of four-legged animals. The child also accommodates or makes changes in previously held knowledge, that is, that there are four-legged animals other than dogs. By acquiring experience, the meaning of words and of language grows richer, and connections between schemata become more complex.

As students learn to read and write independently, the expansion of meaning—the assimilation and accommodation of schemata—takes place on two levels. First, all students possess a broad knowledge base that includes their knowledge of reading and writing skills. On this level, students need to expand their ways of approaching a text and increase their critical thinking as they predict and confirm content. In this way, they learn to activate their prior knowledge about reading and apply it to the acquisition of more sophisticated reading skills.

Activate and Connect

Introduction *(cont.)*

On the second level, students come to their reading with topic-specific knowledge. This knowledge may vary immensely from student to student and population to population, depending on students' prior exposure. Creating and implementing activities that stimulate thinking about a topic will cue students about what they already know. In addition, activities that involve the entire classroom, such as brainstorming or discussion, help ensure that students are on a level playing field when they first approach a particular text. By activating prior knowledge, the schema for that particular concept is brought forward. This activation cues the brain for growth.

Prereading activities also give structure for postreading activities, for example, as students check the text against their predictions. Prereading activities also give a sense of cohesiveness to the classroom community as students work together to create and expand their body of knowledge. Finally, activating prior knowledge promotes curiosity. What more is there to learn? How will learning something new shape and change each student's self-concept and world view? When students are excited about an upcoming text, richer connections are certain to be made as they read. That is the point of reading—to expand one's knowledge and to make one quest to know more.

Strategies for Making Connections

As indicated in the introduction, the strategies for activating prior knowledge range from the simple to the complex. You should select a strategy based on the following:

- **Time allotment:** Will you be spending an afternoon or a week on a particular topic? A simple but effective discussion might be sufficient before reading a brief article on Picasso; but before studying a unit on modern art, you may wish to take students on a trip to the museum.

- **Objective:** If your objective is to encourage discussion and facilitate use of newly introduced vocabulary, then choose a mapping or brainstorming activity. If, on the other hand, you wish readers to be more independent, have students complete an anticipation guide.

- **Previous knowledge:** Students may already know a great deal about the life cycle but may know very little about how a law gets passed through Congress. Be familiar with the prior year's curriculum so that you know which topics you need to spend more time preparing students to approach.

Activate and Connect

Strategy 1: Predicting and Confirming

Begin by having students preview the text and make predictions about the content. Model for students how to create prediction statements and record them on the Predicting and Confirming activity page on page 67. Then, students will read the text with the intention of finding information that either confirms or contradicts their predictions. Students should circle "yes" or "no" in the center column of their activity pages. Finally, students explain the information that confirms or contradicts their predictions. They can include what surprised, confused, or disappointed them about the text information. For example, if students were previewing a text about holidays around the world, they might make predictions about what kinds of celebrations occur on these special days. Students might assume that Boxing Day is related to the sport of boxing. Once they read the text, students will be able to write about the information they learned that supported or disputed their earlier predictions. (Standards 5.1, 5.3)

Strategy 2: Visual Reading Guide

The Visual Reading Guide on page 68 provides struggling readers with a framework for previewing the text features in the reading material. Have students record what they can learn from the various text features (headings, subheadings, graphs, charts, diagrams, illustrations, photographs, and captions) in the left-hand column of the chart. Then students connect the information that they observed with their prior knowledge. For example, in a reading selection on the Revolutionary War, students may encounter a picture of George Washington. Many would record that they knew he was the first president of the United States and that he fought a famous battle at Valley Forge. A careful examination of text features can connect with prior knowledge, which will help students make meaning of the text. (Standards 5.1, 7.6)

Strategy 3: Creating a Prereading Plan

This strategy is used to assess students' depth of understanding of the topic. Use page 69 to have students identify as many words as they can that they associate with the topic. Then ask students to identify how they know these words. Through discussion, students clarify and refine their connections and understanding. You can also ask students to summarize their prior knowledge and identify what they hope to learn from the reading. (Standard 7.6)

Strategy 4: A Scavenger Hunt

Divide students into teams and give each team an identical list of terms and concepts to find. Then, the teams preview the text as quickly as possible to find the term/concept and develop a definition or association based on the text. The first team to finish the scavenger hunt wins. (Standard 5.1)

Activate and Connect

Strategy 5: Previewing and Predicting

Begin by asking students structured questions about their experiences related to the topic of the text. For example, if you are going to read text about sea horses, ask students if they have ever been to an aquarium and seen sea horses. Some students may say yes. Then you can ask them what they observed about sea horses and make a list on the overhead or board. Then, have students preview the text and predict the information that they will learn about sea horses, as well as how it will connect with the list they generated. You can use the Previewing and Predicting activity on page 70 to deliver this lesson. (Standards 5.1, 7.6)

Strategy 6: Previewing and Self-Questioning

Present students with the activity on page 71 to help guide them through the previewing and self-questioning process. Begin by telling students the topic they will be exploring. You may want to show them a picture, colored overhead, or video clip to build intrigue and interest. Then, have students respond to the first question on the right-hand side of the Previewing and Self-Questioning activity page. Students use the questions on the left-hand side of the activity page to preview the text and gather as much information as possible using the text features for guidance. As students read, they complete the remainder of the right side of the activity page, making connections to their prior knowledge and thinking of ways to remember the information. (Standards 5.1, 8.2)

Strategy 7: KWL and KWL Plus

A highly effective strategy, KWL structures students' thinking before and after reading. Often it is difficult to begin this activity without building some background knowledge. You may have students that are ready to jump right in, but if you don't, begin by having students review previous readings connected to the topic of the new article or text they will be reading. For example, if the students are to read about the beginning of the Civil War, you might have them revisit information that they have read about slavery, the political climate, and the president. Then, students put the texts away and as a class, complete the "What do I already know?" portion of the KWL chart (page 72). Work with students to generate questions they have about the topic and complete the center column of the chart. Consider using this as a previewing activity and have students find questions from looking at the headings, subheadings, and pictures in the text. When students are finished reading the text, they should record what they learned and any new questions they may have. As an extension, students reflect on the importance of the information and how they will use or apply what they have learned to their own lives. (Standards 5.1, 5.3, 7.3, 7.6, 8.2) Here's an example of a completed KWL chart about the seasons:

What do I already know?	What do I want to know?	What did I learn?
There are four seasons in a year. Our weather changes with each season. Fall, winter, spring, and summer are all seasons.	What causes seasons? Do all regions have four seasons?	The changing seasons are caused by the changing position of the earth in relation to the sun. Some regions only have two seasons, such as a wet and a dry season.

Activate and Connect

Strategy 8: Anticipation Guides

An anticipation guide is a list of statements pertaining to a particular topic in a piece of text that students are going to read. Before reading, students determine whether or not the statements are true or false or whether or not they agree or disagree with the statements. Students read the text with the intention of confirming their prereading assessment of the statements. After reading, students revisit the statements and identify whether the statements are true or false or whether they agree or disagree based on the text information. Blank anticipation guides are provided for you on pages 73 and 74. Begin by determining the major concepts or themes that you want students to recognize in the text. Determine students' prior knowledge of these concepts and think about whether or not students have any misconceptions. Create statements about the topic/concepts and make sure the statement order follows the text. Students copy these statements into the center column of the anticipation guide. Discuss the statements briefly and have students complete their reading following the anticipation guide procedure. Conduct a follow-up discussion in which you focus on the student beliefs that were changed or confirmed. (Standards 5.3, 7.6) The following example shows some statements that students could identify as true or false while reading a text on George Washington:

Statements About the Topic
George Washington was the first president of the United States.
George Washington lived in the White House while he was president.
George Washington grew up in a very poor family.
George Washington's estate was called Mount Vernon.
He is affectionately known as "the father of his country."
George Washington was named the commander in chief during the Revolutionary War.

Strategy 9: Structured Preview

Some students benefit from an informal preview of text, but others need a more structured approach. Use the Structured Preview activity on page 75 to lead students through the text, making note of text structure, text features, key concepts/facts, predictions, and connections to prior knowledge. A structured approach will help struggling readers tap into their prior knowledge of both reading and life experiences connected to the text. (Standards 5.1, 7.6)

Strategy 10: Semantic Mapping

Semantic mapping can be used in a couple of different ways to connect with prior knowledge. Present students with the Semantic Mapping activity on page 76, and instruct them to record the key concept that they will be reading about in the center circle. Then, students brainstorm everything they know about the topic and create a list on the overhead or board. When students have finished brainstorming, look back at the list to help students determine major categories and record these categories in the outer circles of the semantic maps. Then, students group the listed details under the appropriate categories. You could also have students read, watch a video clip, or listen to an audio recording to create their semantic map. In this case, you would be building students' prior knowledge because you assumed they did not know much about the topic. (Standard 7.6)

Activate and Connect

Strategy 11: Table of Contents

When writing a book, authors may not know much about its topic when they begin. They may construct a table of contents to guide their research. Likewise, you can direct students to a table of contents about a topic. Then have them fill in what they know under each subtopic. For example, if the topic is the tropical rain forest, you might construct the following:

Table of Contents

Location	Rain forests are located in tropical parts of the world.
Climate	Rain forests are very wet.
Geography	The Amazon Rain Forest has a huge river.
Plants	
Animals	There are many birds in the rain forest.
People	
Products	Rubber comes from the rain forest.
Environmental Concerns	Rain forests are disappearing because people need the land to farm.

This activity will activate prior knowledge as well as graphically display what holes students have in their background about a topic. After you have done this strategy with the entire class a few times, students can construct their own table of contents, perhaps in their reading journals. In addition, this activity can help students to summarize their knowledge in an orderly manner once they have completed their reading. Use the activity on page 77 to practice this strategy. (Standards 7.5, 7.6)

Strategy 12: Nonfiction Reading Journal

You may already have your students keeping a response journal of some sort in which they record their personal thoughts about literature. Try using a reading journal with nonfiction text. When you begin a topic, students can write what they know in their nonfiction reading journals. They can also record their predictions in the journal and check them after they read. (See page 78.) (Standards 5.3, 7.6)

Strategy 13: Cloze Frame

This strategy is a great way to activate prior knowlege. Using page 79, have students fill in their thoughts about the text before reading. Then, after they read the text, have students fill in the second half of the page with the new information they have learned. Students can then go back and reread the top half of the sheet to see what was learned from the reading. This is a great strategy to use in small group discussions after the reading. (Standard 7.6)

Activate and Connect

Predicting and Confirming

Directions: Make predictions about what you will learn before you read. As you read, determine whether or not your predictions were confirmed. Then explain using information from the text.

Predictions about the content (What will I learn?)	Confirmed by the text?	Explanation:
	YES NO	
	YES NO	
	YES NO	
	YES NO	
	YES NO	
	YES NO	

Activate and Connect

Visual Reading Guide

Directions: Preview the text and record as many details as you can regarding the text features listed. Then, identify what you already know about the information contained in these text features.

Visual cues or text features	What I already know
Headings:	
Subheadings:	
Bold or italicized words:	
Illustrations, photographs, and captions:	
Charts, graphs, and diagrams:	

Activate and Connect

Creating a Prereading Plan

Directions: Complete the following activities to make a plan for reading about the information.

Topic: _____

Make a list of words that you associate with the topic:

_____

_____

_____

Choose three words from your brainstorming above and record them in the left-hand column of the chart below. Then answer the question in the right-hand column of the chart.

Words	What made you think of this word in connection with the topic?

Write a brief summary of what you already know about the topic: _____

_____

_____

_____

What new information do you hope to learn? _____

_____

_____

_____

Activate and Connect

Previewing and Predicting

Directions: Before you read, preview the text and respond to the questions in each of the columns of the double-entry journal below.

Previewing (before reading)	Predicting (before reading)
What information seems to be significant and important?	Based on your previewing, what do you expect to learn?
Which text features seem important? (captions, charts, graphs, diagrams, maps, photographs, illustrations, headings, subheadings)	How will this information connect to your prior knowledge?

Activate and Connect

Previewing and Self-Questioning

Directions: Preview the text before reading and complete the left-hand column. Before and during reading, answer the questions in the right-hand column.

Previewing (before reading)	Self-Questioning (before and during reading)
What information seems to be significant and important? Which text features seem important? (captions, charts, graphs, diagrams, maps, photographs, illustrations, headings, subheadings)	What information do I already know about the topic? How does the information that I am reading connect to what I already know? How will I remember this information?

Activate and Connect

KWL

Directions: Complete the left-hand and center columns before reading. After reading, complete the right-hand column.

What do I already know?	What do I want to know?	What did I learn?
What I know: How I know:	Questions about the topic:	What I learned: What I still want to learn:

KWL Plus

Reflection: Why is this information important for me to know? How can I use this information?

_____

_____

_____

_____

_____

_____

Activate and Connect

Anticipation Guide (Agree/Disagree)

Directions: Record the statements about the topic in the center of the chart. Before reading, think about whether or not you agree with the statements and place a check in the appropriate box under the "Before Reading" heading. After reading, think about the information you read and whether or not it changed your opinion about any of the statements about the topic. Then, place a check in the appropriate box under the "After Reading" heading.

Before Reading   *After Reading*

Agree	Disagree	Statements about the topic	Agree	Disagree

Activate and Connect

Anticipation Guide (True/False)

Directions: Record the statements about the topic in the center of the chart. Before reading, think about whether or not the statements are true or false and place a check in the appropriate box under the "Before Reading" heading. After reading, think about the information you read and whether or not the statements are true or false. Then, place a check in the appropriate box under the "After Reading" heading.

Before Reading   *After Reading*

True	False	Statements about the topic	True	False

Activate and Connect

Structured Preview

Directions: Preview the text to determine the following elements.

Topic: _____

Text Structure (description, compare/contrast, cause/effect, listing, problem/solution):

_____

Text Features: _____

_____

_____

Key concepts	Facts

Prediction about what I will learn: _____

_____

_____

_____

How will this information connect to what I already know? _____

_____

_____

_____

Activate and Connect

Semantic Mapping

Directions: Use the following semantic map to take notes about the key concept in the center, subtopics in the outer circles, and details on the lines. You will be reading information, watching a movie, listening to an audio tape, or engaging in a class discussion in order to build or tap into your background knowledge about the subject.

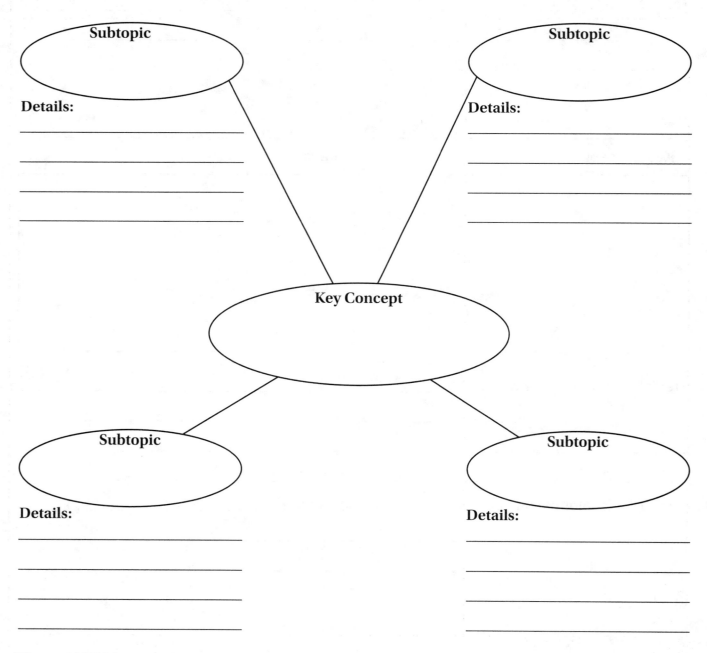

Subtopic

Details:

_____

_____

_____

_____

Subtopic

Details:

_____

_____

_____

_____

Key Concept

Subtopic

Details:

_____

_____

_____

_____

Subtopic

Details:

_____

_____

_____

_____

Activate and Connect

Table of Contents

Directions: Use this sheet to create a table of contents for a nonfiction book or chapter that you are about to read. Fill in what you already know about the topic before you begin reading. Add what you learned when you have finished.

Chapter/Book title	Information I know	Information that I learned

STRATEGIES AND SKILLS

Activate and Connect

Nonfiction Reading Journal

Topic: _____

Source: _____

Pages: _____

Note: Use the back of this sheet to write additional facts or other information.

This topic reminds me of_____.

I know the following facts about this topic:

1. _____

2. _____

3. _____

4. _____

5. _____

I have the following questions about this topic:

1. _____

2. _____

3. _____

I learned the following new facts about this topic:

1. _____

2. _____

3. _____

4. _____

5. _____

I would like to learn more about:

_____

_____

_____

Activate and Connect

Cloze Frame

Prereading Frame

Directions: Before you begin the assigned reading, complete the frame below with thoughts and ideas about what you think the text will be about.

The title of the text is _____.

I think this text will be about _____ and

_____ because _____.

I think the text will answer the following questions:

1. _____

2. _____

3. _____

Postreading Frame

Directions: After you have completed the assigned reading, complete the frame below.

The title of the text is_____.

The text was about _____ and

_____.

I learned the following pieces of information about the topic:

1. _____

2. _____

3. _____

#50469 Successful Strategies

PASSPORT TO COMPREHENSION

Infer
Meaning

#50469 Successful Strategies

Infer Meaning

Introduction

In order to gain meaning from text, students must be able to infer. Inference is the process of judging, concluding, or reasoning based on given information. Strategies for inferring are closely related to those used for visualizing. While visualizing involves mental images, inferring has to do with words and thoughts; when used together, inferring and visualizing strengthen understanding.

Raising Questions

Readers are able to make sound inferences when they are able to blend text information with their prior knowledge. Proficient readers often ask questions that help them to make connections between the text and what they know. Teachers must explicitly teach these skills in order for struggling readers to learn to raise questions and find answers and for proficient readers to be acutely aware of how to strengthen their existing questioning skills. The ability to make inferences develops when readers ask questions such as "How does my prior knowledge help me to understand the text?" and "How does using my visualization techniques help me to create a complete picture of what's going on in the text?"

Making Interpretations and Speculations

When students interpret text meaning, they are tapping into higher-order thinking skills. Questioning, visualizing, and inferring are developmental processes that aid the reader in deepening their interpretations of the text. Proficient readers will examine cause-effect relationships, compare and contrast information, and engage in problem-solving techniques in order to gain more from the text than what is merely on the page. Speculating about future events in the text, implications for the reader, and the importance of text information helps readers to build the foundation for drawing conclusions and making inferences. When students wonder about the text, the benefits include:

- the creation of mental images in order to develop a clearer picture of the text
- linking personal experience and prior knowledge to the text
- heightened engagement with the text
- deeper levels of comprehension
- a greater ability to draw conclusions and make inferences
- an increased appreciation for reading

Reacting

While proficient readers react to text in a variety of ways, struggling readers do not have a mental "tool box" from which to respond to text by making inferences and drawing conclusions. Students need to be explicitly taught how to identify important text information, choose a method for reacting, and link prior knowledge and personal experience to the text. You can aid students with reacting by providing them with a variety of double-entry journal formats, text coding procedures, discussion techniques, opportunities to work with a partner, and ways to use art and drama.

Infer Meaning

Making Observations

Being a critical reader means making observations about text features, text content, and author's choices. Insightful observations provide the groundwork for conclusions and inferences. For example, when a reader can identify specific aspects of a text feature, the likelihood of making critical inferences about the connection between the text feature and the author's purpose or the key concepts that you are trying to teach in the classroom is greatly increased. Some ways to increase students' observational skills include teaching:

- skimming and scanning for specific text features followed by discussion
- skimming and scanning for text content followed by discussion
- silent reading with guiding questions
- buddy reading with guiding questions
- guided reading led by the teacher
- pausing during reading to respond, react, and reflect
- rereading for clarification

Identifying and Assessing Evidence

One of the most effective ways to teach students to identify and assess evidence is to present them with a question, require them to read in order to answer the question, require them to gather text evidence to support the answer to the question, and finally, show them how to assess the validity of the information, the credibility of the sources, and the comprehensiveness of the information.

Using Strategies Independently

Drawing conclusions and making inferences are challenging and sophisticated skills that require intense teacher modeling. Always begin by demonstrating to students how to use the skill. Incorporate think-alouds and think-alongs so that students get to hear your thinking as you draw conclusions and make inferences about text meaning. When you feel that students have developed a certain level of proficiency, allow them to work in groups and with partners to practice the skills. Socialization is highly motivating to students and is an excellent vehicle for providing guided practice toward mastery. Some tips for supporting group work include:

- Make the task very clear by providing step-by-step directions about what you expect from students.
- Assign roles and responsibilities to each group member.
- Require students to "publish" their work, either through oral sharing or a written assignment that will be posted in the classroom.

Once students have had exposure to group work, make sure to provide them with opportunities to use the skills that they have learned independently. Students should be accountable for measurable growth toward the meaningful application of skills.

Infer Meaning

Questions

Students are familiar with being asked questions about a text, but they are probably less familiar with raising questions. Raising their own questions about a text can help students anticipate the types of questions teachers and standardized tests will ask them. Anticipating questions will help students pay attention to and comprehend a text.

The Question-Answer Relationship strategy developed by Taffy Raphael (2005) helps students find answers to questions by analyzing what kinds of questions they are. In this strategy there are three types of questions:

- Right-There questions: The answers to these questions are easy to find. The words in the question are typically phrased exactly like the words in the answer in the text. The words are "right there" and easy to find.
- Think-and-Search questions: The answers to these questions are harder to find, but are in the text. Students will not find the same words in the question as in the answer. The full answer is not always contained in the same sentence.
- On-Your-Own questions: The answers to these questions are not written in the text. Students must use their own knowledge and understanding of the world along with reading the text to find the answer.

The right-there questions are the type of questions to which students may be accustomed, and right-there questions are important for comprehension. However, the think-and-search and on-your-own questions are what inferring is all about. These questions help students to figure out what the author is implying and relate the information to the world.

Strategy 1: Right-There Questions

Students need to practice asking questions. Read a short nonfiction text. Provide a copy of the text for each student. Students, individually or with buddies, write three right-there questions about the text, using page 89. Remind them that the answer should be "right there" with the words in the question. Collect the questions and discuss the questions and their answers with the class as a whole. Verify that all students or teams wrote a right-there question and the answer could easily be found. (Standard 8.2)

Strategy 2: Think-and-Search Questions

Using the same text, follow the procedure from the previous strategy. Students write a think-and-search question using page 90. This activity may be done individually, with buddies, or in small groups. If necessary, the teacher can lead a small group for skill building. Remind students that a think-and-search question's answer can be found in the text, but the answer will not be "right there" with words from the question. Collect questions and discuss answers. Verify that the questions are think-and-search rather than right-there questions. If they are not, discuss why and turn the question into a think-and-search question, using class suggestions. (Standard 8.2)

Infer Meaning

Strategy 3: On-Your-Own Questions

Finally, follow the same procedure as with the previous two strategies, and have the students write on-your-own questions using the activity on page 91. Once again, a small group of students may need to work with the teacher. It is possible that the whole class may need help with this skill at first. If so, conduct this activity as a class and create five on-your-own questions. Let students provide answers to the questions individually or as buddies. Come together as a class and discuss the answers. (Standard 8.2)

Strategy 4: Think-Aloud Questions and Answers

To be effective readers, students must continually raise questions about the text as they read. This process can be presented in a think-aloud method. Read a paragraph or so of a nonfiction text. Think through the process of comprehension. Think of a right-there question you can ask yourself and answer. Think of a think-and-search question you can ask and answer. Finally, think of an on-your-own question that will help with the comprehension of the text. Show students that asking these questions as you read through a text helps them to comprehend the author's meaning. (Standard 8.2)

Strategy 5: Write Your Own Questions

Students try it on their own. Choose a short nonfiction text. Using page 92 for their questions, have students raise questions about the text. They write three right-there questions, two think-and search-questions, and one on-your-own question. Students write only the questions; however, they should know the answers to their questions. (Standard 8.2)

Strategy 6: What Is Implied?

Students must understand that an author does not always directly state all of the information that he or she intends for the reader to comprehend. The author implies some information, and the reader must infer from it. While reading, lead students to look for clues, relate the clues to what they already know, and put all of the information together to figure out what the author means. Have students read through a text as a class, in small groups, or independently and practice finding implied information. Using page 93, they can list the clues from the text, the information they already know, and the inferred information gained by putting all the information together. (Standard 7.6)

Strategy 7: Making Observations

Read a short, nonfiction text with the whole class. Then break students into heterogeneous groups to make observations on the text. Each group should make at least ten observations and then rate them in importance. Students can use page 94 to record their observations. Each group can choose who will write and who will report the information. Come together as a class to compare observations. (Standard 7.6)

Infer Meaning

Strategy 8: Reactions to Nonfiction Text

Break up the class into small, heterogeneous, cooperative groups. Make sure each group has a competent reader, a competent writer, and someone who will keep the group on task. Also make sure that the group of students will work well together. Assign a job to each student in the group. There can be a Relater (the reader), a Recorder (the writer), a Manager (the task keeper), and a Reporter (someone who reports the group's reactions). Assign all groups the same nonfiction text to read. The Relater reads the article to the group. Then the group will discuss their reactions to the text. The Recorder writes all of the reactions on a copy of page 95. The Manager can make sure that all members state their reactions while he or she watches the clock to allow everyone time to talk before time is up. Finally, when the groups reconvene, the Reporter will present the reactions to the class. Afterward, have a class discussion about the similarities and differences of the different groups' reactions. Remind the class to respect and value all the reactions of their classmates. (Standard 7.6)

Strategy 9: One Picture Is Worth a Thousand Words

Asking the right questions can get students to think "outside the box" and stretch their inferring skills to observe and make speculations. Duplicate and distribute copies of page 96. Explain to students that first they are to work alone for about ten minutes by looking at the picture and answering the questions. After their time is up, have students move into pairs or small groups to compare and revise their answers. Emphasize to students that they don't have to change their answers if they disagree with their partner(s). If they can adequately defend their reasoning when asked, it can be considered a "correct" answer. (Standards 5.3, 7.6, 8.2)

Strategy 10: Making Inferences about Characters

Students can use the activity on page 97 for this strategy. Students choose a character from the text and record his or her actions on one side of the page and inferences about how the character felt as a result of those actions or events on the other side of the page. Students should also think about how they would feel in the same or a similar situation. (Standard 7.6)

Strategy 11: Making Inferences about Concepts

Teaching students to use concept-based principles is the most highly effective way to help them retain factual information. Make sure to identify the concept that you want students to learn throughout the course of the unit. Present students with guiding questions that will help them to categorize and make sense of the vast amounts of information that they will be learning. Present them with the activity on page 98 and have them record facts from the text on the left and their inferences on the right. Be sure to model for students how to make their inferences connect to their conceptual understandings and the guiding questions that they have been exploring. (Standard 7.6)

Strategy 12: Using Vocabulary to Make Inferences

Students use the chart on page 99 to make inferences about the meanings of unknown words in the text that they are reading. Students then check their ability to make inferences by looking up the words in a dictionary. This activity works well in small groups, in pairs, or individually. (Standard 5.5)

Infer Meaning

Strategy 13: Making Speculations

Students read a text in a small group, with a buddy, or individually, and make three speculations about it. They have to include at least two pieces of information either from the text or from their prior knowledge about the topic to support their speculation. For some classes it may be beneficial to do this activity as a class and lead the class through the process the first time (or two times). Students can complete the task individually when they are ready, using the activity on page 100. This activity can be done with more than one text. (Standard 7.5)

Strategy 14: Drawing Conclusions

Guiding students through the process of drawing conclusions will ensure that they develop proficiency in this area. Two ideas include drawing conclusions about an issue (page 101) and drawing conclusions about the author's intent (page 102). The example below shows how students may draw conclusions about an issue:

> *Issue or problem:* Homework helps all kids learn more and teaches them to be responsible; yet, some teachers give a lot of homework and some teachers don't give any homework.

> *Proposed Solution:* All teachers should be required to give homework. Teachers in the same grade must give a similar amount of homework to students.

> *Pros:* This solution would make it fair because all students would have to do homework.

> > Homework for every student means that all students expect homework and will have to learn to be responsible and complete and return each assignment.

> > Homework is a good way for parents to see what their kids are doing in school and be involved in their education.

> *Cons:* Students can be very busy after school with extracurricular activities, and homework can often cause stress and frustration after a long day.

> > Not all students have the same skills, so homework can be very easy for some students and very difficult for others.

> > Some parents are not at home to help students when they aren't able to do their homework on their own.

When examining the author's intent, have students examine the main topic, subtopics, text structure, text features, and language choices. Careful observations about these aspects of the text will help students to draw a logical conclusion about the author's intent. After students complete this process, consider dividing them into partners and role-playing a discussion about the author's intent. One student takes on the role of the author, and the other student assumes the role of the reader. (Standard 7.5)

Infer Meaning

Right-There Questions

Directions: Read the text below, and then read the three sample questions that follow.

> A frog lays eggs. The frog's eggs hatch into tadpoles. As the tadpoles quickly mature, they grow and lose body parts. The tadpoles grow front legs, grow back legs, and lose their tails. One day, "Splash!" and no more tadpole.

Sample 1: Right-There Question: What do the frog's eggs hatch into?

Sample 2: Think-and-Search Question: As a tadpole matures, what does it lose?

Sample 3: On-Your-Own Question: What happens to the tadpole at the end of the text?

Now it is your turn. With a partner or by yourself, read the text your teacher has given you. Think of three right-there questions. Remember, the answer to the right-there question is in the same sentence as the question words. You do not have to write the answers to the questions, but you should know the answers and they should be easily found in the text.

Question 1: _____

_____

_____

Question 2: _____

_____

_____

Question 3: _____

_____

_____

Infer Meaning

Think-and-Search Questions

Directions: Read the text below, and then read the three sample questions that follow.

A frog lays eggs. The frog's eggs hatch into tadpoles. As the tadpoles quickly mature, they grow and lose body parts. The tadpoles grow front legs, grow back legs, and lose their tails. One day, "Splash!" and no more tadpole.

Sample 1: Right-There Question: What do the frog's eggs hatch into?

Sample 2: Think-and-Search Question: As a tadpole matures, what does it lose?

Sample 3: On-Your-Own Question: What happens to the tadpole at the end of the text?

Now it is your turn. With a partner or by yourself, read the text your teacher has given you. Think of two think-and-search questions. Remember, the answer to the think-and-search question is not in the same sentence as the question words. The reader must think and search for the answer. You do not have to write the answers to the questions, but you should know the answers, and they should be easily found in the text.

Question 1: _____

_____

_____

Question 2: _____

_____

_____

Infer Meaning

On-Your-Own Questions

Directions: Read the text below, and then read the three sample questions.

A frog lays eggs. The frog's eggs hatch into tadpoles. As the tadpoles quickly mature, they grow and lose body parts. The tadpoles grow front legs, grow back legs, and lose their tails. One day, "Splash!" and no more tadpole.

Sample 1: Right-There Question: What do the frog's eggs hatch into?

Sample 2: Think-and-Search Question: As a tadpole matures, what does it lose?

Sample 3: On-Your-Own Question: What happens to the tadpole at the end of the text?

Now it is your turn. With a partner or by yourself, read the text your teacher has given you. Think of one On-Your-Own question. Remember, the reader must use his or her own knowledge and understanding of the world, along with reading the text, to find the answer. You do not have to write the answer to the question, but you should know the answer.

Question: _____

_____

_____

Infer Meaning

Write Your Own Questions

Directions: Read the text your teacher has provided. Compose three right-there questions, two think-and-search questions, and one on-your-own question. Remember to write only the question, not the answer, but know the answer to the questions that you have written.

Types of Questions

- **Right-There:** The answers to these questions are easy to find. The words in the question are typically phrased exactly like the words in the answer in the text. The words are "right there" and easy to find.

- **Think-and-Search:** The answers to these questions are harder to find, but are in the text. Students will not find the same words in the question as in the answer. The full answer is not always contained in the same sentence.

- **On-Your-Own:** The answers to these questions are not written in the text. Students must use their own knowledge and understanding of the world, along with reading the text, to find the answer.

Title: _____

Right-There Question 1: _____

_____

Right-There Question 2: _____

_____

Right-There Question 3: _____

_____

Think-and-Search Question 1: _____

_____

Think-and-Search Question 2: _____

_____

On-Your-Own Question: _____

_____

Infer Meaning

What Is Implied?

Directions: Read the text that your teacher has given you. Discuss with your class, in a small group, or with a partner any information the author has not directly stated but has implied. Write the inference you have made. Write two clues and any previous knowledge that you have that led you to infer the author's meaning.

Title: _____

Inference: _____

_____

_____

Clues:

1. _____

_____

_____

2. _____

_____

_____

Previous knowledge: _____

_____

_____

Infer Meaning

Making Observations

Group members: _____

Directions: After listening to the text read by your teacher, record your group's observations on the lines below. After your group has made at least ten observations, decide the order of importance of these observations. Which observation is most important to the comprehension of the text? That observation will be numbered 1. The next most important observation will be 2, and so on. Put the number of importance in the box at the beginning of each observation. When all groups have finished, compare answers to see if you rated the observations at the same level of importance.

Observation: ☐ _____

_____

Observation: ☐ _____

_____

Observation: ☐ _____

_____

Observation: ☐ _____

_____

Observation: ☐ _____

_____

Observation: ☐ _____

_____

Observation: ☐ _____

_____

Observation: ☐ _____

_____

Observation: ☐ _____

_____

Observation: ☐ _____

_____

Infer Meaning

Reactions to Nonfiction Text

Group Members

The Relater: _____

The Recorder: _____

The Manager: _____

The Reporter: _____

Directions: Listen closely as the "relater" reads the text that your teacher assigned. The three other members of the group can jot down their reactions on scratch paper. When the relater has finished reading, the "manager" will call on members one at a time to give a reaction. The manager will allow the "recorder" time to write down the reaction before moving to the next member. Finally, meet with the whole class, and the "reporter" will report the reactions of the group.

Title of text: _____

Reactions:

Member 1: _____

_____

_____

Member 2: _____

_____

_____

Member 3: _____

_____

_____

Member 4: _____

_____

_____

Infer Meaning

One Picture Is Worth a Thousand Words

Directions: Carefully look over the details of this picture. Answer the questions in complete sentences on a separate piece of paper. Be prepared to defend your answers.

1. What meal is the table set for?

2. How many family members are there?

3. Which family member sits in which chair?

4. How can you tell if the baby is a boy or a girl?

5. Is someone in the family left-handed? Who is it, and how can you tell?

6. What is everyone drinking?

7. How old do you think the father is? Which is reasonable: 18 years, 35 years, or 56 years? Why do you say so?

8. What type of job does the father have?

9. Does the family have a pet? What is it? How do you know?

10. What chores do you think the children might have? How do you know?

Infer Meaning

Making Inferences about Characters

Directions: Choose a character from the text. Record his or her actions on the left side of the page, and record inferences that you make about his or her feelings and reactions on the right side of the page. Make sure to respond to the personal experience question included on the right side of the page.

Character's actions (text information)	Inferences
What were the actions of the character in the text?	How did the character feel as a result of his or her actions or the events that happened? Why?
What were the events that happened to the character in the text?	Would you have felt the same as the character in the text? Why or why not?

Infer Meaning

Making Inferences about Concepts

Directions: Use the following activity page to make inferences about the facts you are learning and their connection to the larger concept.

Concept Being Studied: _____

Guiding Questions: _____

_____

_____

Facts from the text	Inferences (How do these facts connect to the larger concept? How do these facts help you to answer the guiding questions?)

Infer Meaning

Using Vocabulary to Make Inferences

Directions: Use the following chart to make inferences about the meanings of unknown words in the text you are reading.

Unknown vocabulary word	Inference about meaning	Dictionary definition	Correct inference?
			YES NO
			YES NO
			YES NO
			YES NO
			YES NO
			YES NO

Infer Meaning

Making Speculations

Directions: Read the text your teacher has given you for this assignment. Think about what you read in order to speculate on the future of the topic or other topics. List at least two items of information that support your speculation.

Example: The school cafeteria has a limited supply of food for this month. They will be able to serve hamburgers, corndogs, chicken patties, and peanut butter sandwiches. They also have apples, oranges, and milk.

Sample speculation: Next month there will be more choices at the cafeteria.

Support: The text says there is a limited supply this month, and maybe next month there will be more of a selection.

Food doesn't store forever, and new supplies have to come in.

Title: _____

What the text is about in my (our) own words: _____

_____

_____

Speculation 1: _____

_____

_____

Support: _____

_____

Speculation 2: _____

_____

_____

Support: _____

_____

Infer Meaning

Drawing Conclusions about an Issue

Directions: Use this graphic organizer to draw a conclusion about the issue.

Issue or problem:

Proposed solution:

Pros	Cons

Conclusion: Draw a conclusion about the best course of action and provide reasoning and support for your decision.

Infer Meaning

Drawing Conclusions about the Author's Intent

Directions: Respond to the following prompts and questions in order to draw a conclusion about the author's intent.

Title of the text: _____

Main topic: _____

Important subtopics: _____

_____

_____

Text structure selected: _____

Text features included: _____

_____

Words or phrases that reveal the author's beliefs or opinion about the topic:

_____

_____

Conclusion about the author's purpose (What does the author want the reader to gain from reading the information?):

_____

_____

_____

_____

_____

_____

_____

Passport to Comprehension

Ask Questions

Ask Questions

Introduction

What is the difference between an active reader and a passive one?

Active, skilled readers approach nonfiction text with questions such as "What is the meaning of the title?" and "What type of text is this?" They pursue the answers to questions as they read, such as "What does the author mean by this statement?" Finally, they think beyond the text with more questions after they have finished reading; for example, "Where can I find additional facts?" Their active questioning leads them to the next piece of text, the next piece of information. Through questioning, learning becomes an ongoing process.

Passive readers, on the other hand, may not realize that their comprehension might be improved by forming their own questions as they read. Passive readers miss making rich connections between the text and their personal experiences, as well as those within the text, when they do not ask questions. Each reading assignment becomes a dead end rather than an invitation.

To turn passive readers into active ones, teachers need to model not only the process of questioning but also an enthusiastic embrace of the process. Teachers must also model different types of questions. There are questions that require a simple factual answer, questions that require critical thinking, and even questions that may never be answered, e.g., "Why does every living thing eventually die?"

In addition to modeling, teachers must give students skills to generate questions on their own. Some methods, such as brainstorming, are freewheeling ways for students to form questions. Other methods, such as journalistic questioning, give students a systematic way of creating useful questions.

Good questions engage a student's curiosity, encourage original thinking, assess a student's ability to recall and infer, and even prompt additional questions. Good questions excite and motivate reading. They propose and predict ideas. They help readers check for understanding. They beg for answers and are not easily brushed aside.

This section will aid the teacher in producing effective questions. It will also provide strategies for teaching students how to use questions to read with purpose, to check understanding during reading, and to formulate additional questions. As in previous sections, there are strategies for the teacher's own use, strategies to teach to students, and accompanying activity pages. Be flexible, however, in applying strategies to all phases of reading.

Ask Questions

Awareness of Proficient Reading Strategies

Questions are extremely motivating to student learners because it is a natural human inclination to want to understand and make sense of the world. When it comes to reading, questioning strategies can help arouse curiosity, provide direction for research, formulate a purpose for reading, and stimulate further reading and investigation about a topic.

In an educational climate driven by assessment and accountability, it is important to understand the difference between assessment questions and genuine learning questions. Assessment questions are those questions that we already know the answer to and that we use to measure the academic achievement of students. Genuine learning questions are those questions that we don't know the answers to, arouse our curiosity, and require further inquiry on the part of both the teacher and the student. There is a place in the classroom for both kinds of questions, and it is essential that students become proficient at using reading strategies that allow them to answer both kinds of questions successfully and confidently.

Categorizing and Differentiating Among Questions

Categorizing questions helps readers to differentiate among a variety of purposes for reading. Understanding and applying such strategies can aid readers in knowing the kinds of reading and thinking that they have to do in order to answer a question proficiently. The skill of categorizing is one that is useful both in school and various real-world contexts. When applied to reading and questioning, categorizing skills are highly valuable and integral to success in many life situations.

Monitoring Comprehension

Teachers must model strategies so that there is a gradual release of responsibility to the students for strategy use. Students must have access to a variety of strategies in order to clarify, revise, and reformulate their initial understandings of text content. There are two types of explicit modeling (Roehler and Duffy 1991) that can ensure that students move toward taking responsibility for monitoring their reading comprehension: talk-alouds and think-alouds. In a talk-aloud, present students with the components of a particular monitoring strategy and then orally lead them through these steps by questioning and showing students how to apply the strategy to a particular piece of text. It is particularly useful to make an overhead transparency of the text and the steps of the strategy to share with students. As you lead students through the strategy, appropriately mark the text on the overhead to demonstrate exactly how to apply the strategy.

Think-alouds (Meichenbaum, Burland, Gruson, and Cameron 1985) require the teacher to present the steps of the strategy and then share with students the actual thinking that accompanies the use of this strategy. This thinking may include confusion, misconceptions, general wonderings, and discovery. It is important to show students that you, as an adult reader, also have to wonder, clarify, and question in order to come to an understanding of text information.

Ask Questions

Organizing Content Knowledge

The amount of information that students need to make sense of is overwhelming. Therefore, it is imperative that they be taught ways to organize content knowledge. One effective method is to focus your instruction around concept-based learning. The following are some basic questions that you can ask yourself when planning a unit:

1. What is the major concept being investigated or studied?

2. What are the guiding questions that will help students make sense of this topic?

3. What texts will I use to help students find answers to the guiding questions?

4. How will I help students organize the information that they find in order to maximize their content knowledge and its connections to the major concept?

Before, During, and After

In order for students to become truly proficient readers, they must understand that reading is a process and that there are specific behaviors to engage in before, during, and after reading. Questioning skills must be developed at each stage of the reading process, and these questions can focus on either the content of the text or the process of reading. The following questions can be shared with students to guide their thinking before, during, and after reading.

Before
- What do I already know about the topic?
- What does the title reveal about the topic or content of the text?
- What strategies do I know that could help me make sense of the text?

During
- What new information have I learned that clarifies my original understanding of the topic?
- What strategies can I use to monitor my comprehension of the information that I am learning and its connection to major concepts?

After
- What is my overall understanding of the topic?
- What strategy was most effective in making sense of the information?

Ask Questions

Connecting Prior Knowledge

Questions that connect students to their prior knowledge are essential for constructing meaning. The following is a step-by-step process for connecting prior knowledge to the content learned during daily instruction. Post the following questions on a chart or on the board to help guide students throughout their learning experiences in your classroom.

1. What do I already know about the topic?

2. What relevant text information have I read?

3. How does the text connect to what I know?

4. How does the connection further my understanding of the topic?

Reflective questions such as these will help to build students' metacognitive abilities and make them proficient readers.

Making Inferences

Making inferences is yet another real-world skill that individuals need in many real-world contexts. When reading, it is important that students know the questions that they should be asking in order to make sense of the written text, which contains explicit information, and the unwritten text, which resides in their personal experiences and prior knowledge, and is often implicitly referenced in the text. The following are some questions that students can ask themselves in order to build this skill:

1. What conclusions can I draw based on information in the text?

2. What predictions can I make by looking at headings, subheadings, and pictures?

3. How does my prior knowledge help me to make reasonable inferences?

Using Strategies Independently

The following strategies will help build students' proficiencies as readers. Adapt these strategies to suit the needs of your classroom. Remember the gradual release of responsibility. It is essential that students learn to use these strategies independently. This independence is achieved through teacher modeling, direct instruction, think-alouds, and the expectation that students will internalize the modeling and apply the strategies they have learned to their own reading.

Strategy 1: Question Games

Make your classroom an environment that honors inquiry and investigation. Divide students into teams and ask general questions from such games as Trivial Pursuit and Brain Quest. Allow students a day to research various topics of interest and generate their own questions that can be used for cooperative games to answer knowledge-based questions. Gradually incorporate questions from topics and concepts that students are learning in your classroom. Later in the school year, make sure to include questions that require students to make inferences, draw conclusions, and extend their thinking. (Standard 8.2)

Ask Questions

Strategy 2: Question of the Day

Another technique that shows the importance of inquiry is starting a "question of the day." Begin with general questions about current events, personal experiences, and activities happening within the school. Invite students to generate the questions of the day. Before you officially begin class each day, have students answer the questions and discuss them briefly. Gradually begin integrating questions that deal with topics or concepts learned in class. Use a variety of simple and complex questions. (Standard 8.2) Here are some examples that might help to get the routine started:

- What is going on in the news that is interesting or surprising?
- Did this morning feel like the start of a good or bad day? Why?
- What did you learn from yesterday's assembly?
- How would you improve the playground here at school?
- What is the title of a book that you are reading that you think others might enjoy? Why?
- What makes a good friend?
- Has there ever been a time when you were wrong and you said that you were sorry?
- What famous American who we read about yesterday helped free slaves? Why was she brave?
- How many words do you know that are related to geometry?
- How are alligators and crocodiles similar and different?

Strategy 3: Question Web

Question webs (page 113) are a great way for students to gather information about one specific question. These questions can be student- or teacher-generated. Students record their question in the center of the web. Then they read and research the answers to the question by accessing a variety of resources. Students are particularly motivated if they can work as a team to gather information in order to answer the question at the center of the web. After they have gathered enough information, they may work together to synthesize what they have learned into a coherent response. Students will need you to model the synthesis of information gained. Have a sample question web on large butcher paper and then use two highlighters to code essential and extraneous information. Demonstrate for students how to blend, combine, and connect the essential information into a response to the question. (Standard 8.2)

Strategy 4: Question/Answer Relationships (QAR)

Teaching students to understand question/answer relationships can greatly aid their ability to answer questions proficiently. By using this strategy, you will teach students that there are "in the text" questions (right-there, think-and-search) and "in my head" questions (author-and-me, on-my-own). Use the activity sheet on page 114 to guide students through the identification of questions. Then have students read a particular piece of text and use the appropriate code to apply their knowledge of QAR. (Standard 8.2)

Ask Questions

Strategy 4: Question/Answer Relationships (QAR) *(cont.)*

If the students are reading a biography of Elizabeth Cady Stanton and Susan B. Anthony, they could connect the following codes to each question:

Right-There: What did Stanton and Anthony do to change the country?

Think-and-Search: How did life in America change after the Seneca Falls Convention in 1848?

Author-and-Me: Why were the actions of these women so bold and courageous?

On-My-Own: Why do you think Elizabeth Cady Stanton and Susan B. Anthony were such good friends?

Strategy 5: Stance Questioning

Stance questioning is a way to gain a picture of where the reader "stands" in relation to the text. When readers "enter" into text, they begin to form a global understanding of the text. As they "move" through the text, they develop their interpretations and further their initial understandings. As they "exit" the text, they are able to relate personal experiences and prior knowledge to the text information. When readers have fully "exited" the text and gained some distance, they are able to analyze the author's decisions (Langer 1987). Use the activity sheet on page 115 to allow students to choose questions to guide them as they move through the reading process. (Standards 7.6, 8.2)

Strategy 6: Double-Entry Journal

Double-entry journals make the metacognitive process of proficient reading explicitly clear. Instruct students to simply divide their notebook paper in half and record text information on the left-hand side and their reflections, questions, and/or responses on the right-hand side. This strategic tool teaches students that they are not merely reading words, but that their brains should be actively making note of both the text and the thinking that goes on in relation to the text. Have students read content-related text and use the Double-Entry Journal on page 116 to exercise their metacognitive skills. (Standard 7.6)

Strategy 7: Question Builder Chart

Students will begin by listing random, unconnected questions about a given topic. As their reading and questioning skills improve, encourage them to build their questions so that each answer creates a deeper understanding of the topic or concept under investigation. Have students use the Question Builder Chart on page 117 during or after reading to record significant text information and then reflect on that text information by responding to the sentence starters on the right side of the chart. (Standard 8.2)

Strategy 8: Journalistic Questions

Journalistic questions—those questions that begin with who, what, where, when, why, and how—can certainly be used any time during an assigned reading. Also known as 5W+H questions (Who, What, Where, When, Why, and How), students should commit these to memory so that they can be recalled readily whenever they need a little structure for generating questions. Extend the concept by discussing the fact that there may be more than one question for each question word. You may use page 118 to initiate a discussion and guide students in using 5W+H questions for their reading. (Standard 8.2)

Ask Questions

Strategy 9: Question Jar

Keep a jar labeled "Questions" and slips of paper nearby for students to anonymously jot down questions to which they want answers but are too embarrassed to ask aloud. This jar is where students can ask those proverbial "dumb" questions that they believe they should already know the answers to but don't. Sometimes these questions will clue you to some skill or concept that students are missing. Make sure that students know that the question jar is there for questions related to the content that is being studied so that it does not become a repository for "Dear Abby" types of questions. Answer students' questions on a daily or weekly basis. Refer the questions that are not easily answered to an individual student or a committee, or have students look up the answer in various resources as part of the next library or computer lab trip. (Standard 8.2)

Strategy 10: Question of the Week

Designate a spot on your board/bulletin board for posting the Question of the Week. In this way, you remind yourself and your students to maintain curiosity and openness to discovery. You will find a list of thought-provoking questions on page 119, but you can also generate questions in the following ways:

- Focus on a weekly theme in the content areas.

- Focus on questions based on a different type of text or resource each week.

- Ask students to generate questions (see Strategy 9: Question Jar, above).

- Focus on current events in the community, the nation, or the world.

- Focus on historical and/or scientific figures.

- Focus on mathematical concepts.

Perhaps midway through the year, students will be ready to write questions for each other for the Question of the Week. (Standards 7.6, 8.2)

Strategy 11: Little Snapshot Questions, Big Picture Questions

This strategy is a simple way to get students to think about all types of questions. Snapshot questions can be thought of as those questions that can be answered in a flash, or that capture a small nugget of information when they are answered. Big picture questions can be thought of as those that pull the camera back so that a maximum amount of information is captured. Brainstorm questions with students before or after reading a text, and then work with them to sort out which questions ask for snapshots of information and which require them to pull back and think about the big picture. Chances are that there will be plenty of the former questions but few of the latter type of questions, as the latter requires more abstract thinking. Model big picture questions and point them out when you find them in textbooks and other resources. As an extended activity, use the questions on page 120 to initiate a discussion. (Standard 8.2)

Ask Questions

Strategy 12: Question Lists

Begin by having students preview the text and generate as many questions as possible on the board or on large butcher paper. Then, read the text aloud with students, pausing during reading to record more questions on the class list. After reading, record any final questions. Then go through the list and discuss the questions, placing a code of "A" next to any questions that were answered explicitly in the text. Discuss the remaining questions and how conceptual knowledge or inferences are needed to answer these questions. (Standard 5.1)

Strategy 13: Big and Small Questions

Provide students with large and small sticky notes. Instruct them to read the text information and record questions (on the big sticky notes) that require making inferences, referencing concept knowledge, connecting to other texts or information learned, or researching further. Essentially, students are capturing the "big" ideas on the big sticky notes. Instruct students to record fact-based questions, right-there questions, and questions about vocabulary on the little sticky notes, which are intended to represent smaller ideas. After reading, create a T-chart on the board labeled "Big" on the left side and "Small" on the right side. Students put their sticky notes in the correct column. Discuss whether or not the questions are "correct" in that they do represent big and small ideas. Students can come up to the board and choose a sticky note to which they will respond, either orally or in writing. (Standards 7.6, 8.2)

Strategy 14: Keeping Track of "Big" Questions

It is often helpful for students to keep track of the questions that they have about the topic of the text. Students often have questions both before and after reading. Using the chart on page 121, students can write these questions and the key ideas that they learn from the text. This helps students to focus what they think about as they read. (Standards 7.6, 8.2)

Strategy 15: Fact Connector Chart

A great questioning strategy is to have students record facts from their reading and then think of how the information that was read connects to the key topic or concept. Students should also think about how key facts are related to each other. Asking questions to connect the key facts helps students make sense of their reading and how it relates to a bigger idea. Use the chart on page 122 with this activity. (Standard 7.5)

Strategy 16: Questioning Squares

As students read, they should ask questions about what they are reading. Sometimes these questions can be asked of oneself, sometimes they can be asked of the author, and other times they can be asked of the teacher or other classmates. Using the chart on page 123, students can record key information from their reading and then think of questions for these different audiences. (Standards 7.5, 8.2)

Ask Questions

Question Web

Directions: Write your question in the center circle. Record your answers on the outer spokes of the web.

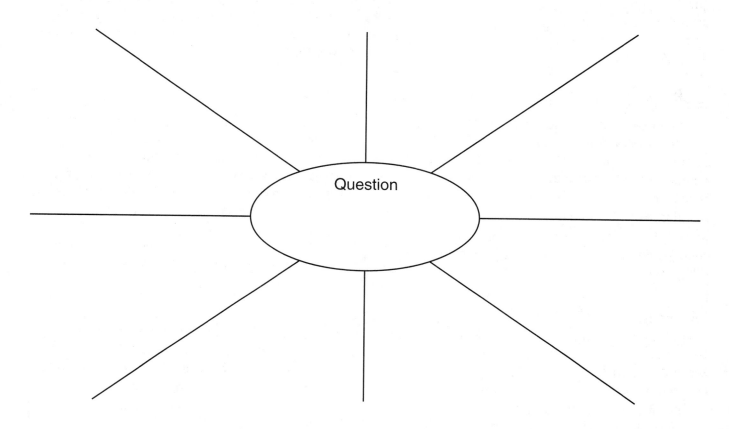

Question

Synthesis of information: Use the most important text information that you gained to write a response to the question at the center of your web.

_____

_____

_____

_____

_____

_____

_____

Ask Questions

Question/Answer Relationships

Directions: Read the following information aloud. Observe the differences among each of these four kinds of questions.

In the text	In my head
Right-There The answer to the question can be found easily and immediately in the text. The words used to create the question are the same words found in the text.	**Author-and-Me** The answer to the question is not found directly in the text. The reader has to think about the information that the author provided, prior knowledge about the topic, and personal experience. The reader has to make connections in order to answer the question.
Think-and-Search The answer to the question can be found in the text, but the reader may have to combine two or more parts of the text to arrive at an answer. The words in the question may not directly lead the reader to the answer in the text. The reader has to make connections in order to arrive at an answer.	**On-My-Own** The answer to the question is not found in the text. The reader must use prior knowledge and personal experiences to answer the question. The reader may even be able to answer the question without having read the text, although text information will enhance the response.

Use the following codes to identify the kinds of questions you are being asked:

R = Right-There

T = Think-and-Search

A = Author-and-Me

O = On-My-Own

Ask Questions

Stance Questioning

Directions: Respond to the following questions in order to develop your understanding of the text.

Global Understanding—Being out and stepping into the text

- What is the overall purpose of the text?

- What is the most important point in the text?

- What details support the most important point?

- How do the text features help support the main idea of the text?

Developing an Interpretation—Being in and moving through the text

- When were you able to infer the feelings or attitudes of any of the people described in the text?

- When were you able to relate concepts or themes to specific information in the text?

- When were you able to compare two excerpts of significant information from the text?

- When were you able to identify the cause/effect relationship of important events, concepts, or ideas in the text?

- How would the information be different if one of the events or steps described was changed or deleted?

Reflecting on Personal Experiences—Being in and stepping out of the text

- What prior knowledge/personal experience can you connect to this topic?

- How is the author's point of view on this topic similar or different than your point of view?

- What other information would you like to learn on this topic?

- What new information have you gained about this topic, and why is this information important to you?

Critical Response—Stepping out and analyzing the reading experience

- How does the author create interest about his/her subject?

- Based on the text, what kind of teacher would the author make? Give specific examples.

- What does the author believe about his/her subject? How do you know?

Ask Questions

Double-Entry Journal

Directions: As you read, record significant information from the text and your questions about what you have read. Use the following sentence and question starters to get you started with your questions:

I don't understand when…

Why did…?

I'm confused about…

How did…?

Quote, summary, or illustration	Questions and wonderings

Ask Questions

Question Builder Chart

Directions: Read the text and record key information by copying a significant quote or summarizing important information. Then use the question starters to build your understanding of the concepts or ideas about which you are learning.

Quote or summary of text information	Questions
	I was confused when… I want to understand the information about… Because… I wonder if… As I continue reading, I most want to know about…

Ask Questions

Journalistic Questions

Journalists ask many questions in order to get the information they need to write a story. The basic set of questions consists of the 5Ws+H, but look at all the questions that can be generated by thinking about the following six words:

- **Who?**

Examples: Whom is the story about? Whom did it affect? Who caused the problem? Who solved the problem? Who cares (or doesn't care) about the problem? Who spoke? Who voted? Who observed or witnessed the event?

- **What?**

Examples: What happened? What caused it to happen? What is new or different? What has remained the same? What might happen? What do people want to make happen? What do people want to prevent from happening?

- **Where?**

Examples: Where does the story take place? Where is the event going to happen? Where might the same thing happen? Where could this only happen?

- **When?**

Examples: When did the story did place? When will the event happen? When will the event happen again? When will the event stop? When is the person going (or returning)?

- **Why?**

Examples: Why did this problem happen? Why are people upset (or happy or confused or . . .)? Why did something work? Why didn't something work? Why is (or isn't) it someone's fault?

- **How?**

Examples: How can the problem be fixed? How can the problem be prevented? How could this event occur? How can people (or animals) behave this way? How long (or short or big or small) is it?

Journalistic questions are useful for writing articles and reports, but they can be used to help you brainstorm anytime you have a reading or writing task to complete. Try to remember 5Ws+H whenever you need to make up a set of questions. As you write each beginning word, try to let your mind float free so that all possible questions come to mind. Then decide which questions are the most useful or interesting ones and focus on those.

Ask Questions

Question of the Week

Directions: Post this list of questions in a designated spot on the board or on a bulletin board, or follow the suggestions in Strategy 10: Question of the Week for generating your own questions.

- Where do escalators go?
- What makes food spicy?
- What is a computer chip made from?
- Who invented waffles?
- How do coal engines work?
- Why does sand extinguish a fire?
- What are dragonfly nymphs?
- What is carrageen gum made of?
- How do we see colors?
- What is a protozoa?
- Who invented SCUBA equipment?
- What is continental drift?
- Who was the first animal in space?
- How far away is Lima, Peru?
- Who was Sigmund Freud?
- Is Pluto a planet?
- Do parrots mate for life?
- How do ants communicate?
- What makes a watch tick?
- How high is Earth's atmosphere?
- What are neurons?
- What is juvenile diabetes?

- What is antidisestablishmentarianism?
- Why is a foot 12 inches?
- What is the meaning of "ricochet"?
- Who was Susan B. Anthony?
- What is the poem on the Statue of Liberty?
- Who were the members of the Donner party?
- How is milk made?
- What American Indian tribe makes kachinas?
- What does the liver do?
- Who invented backgammon?
- Where do tamarind trees grow?
- How do swallows make nests?
- Which California mission is the "Queen of Missions"?
- What African nation was once known as the Belgian Congo?
- What is an empanada?
- Who invented nylon?
- Who wrote "Blue Danube"?
- How is sugar carmelized?
- Where do mangos come from?

Ask Questions

Little Snapshot Questions, Big Picture Questions

Directions: With a partner, decide upon a historic or scientific person who would make an interesting talk show guest. Together, you will need to decide upon the questions that the "host" needs to ask this prominent guest. Sample questions are provided here. You can use these or write your own.

Note: Be sure to write the resources for your answers on the back of this sheet or on a separate sheet of paper.

Who is the famous person who will appear on the show?

_____

What is the remarkable event or discovery that led to wanting to have this particular "guest" on the show?

_____

Sample questions:

1. What events led up to the remarkable occurrence or discovery?

_____

_____

2. What obstacles did the famous person have to overcome?

_____

_____

3. Who supported the famous person in his or her trials and tribulations?

_____

_____

4. What enemies or foes did the famous person face?

_____

_____

5. If the famous person had it to do all over again, would he or she do so?

_____

_____

6. What advice does the famous person have for the "audience"?

_____

_____

7. What will be the famous person's next move?

_____

_____

Ask Questions

Keeping Track of "Big" Questions

Directions: Use the top part of the following chart to record questions about the topic before you start reading. Read the text and record the key ideas in the middle part of the chart. Then refine, revise, or add questions in the bottom part of the chart.

Questions before reading:

Key ideas from the text:

Questions after reading:

Ask Questions

Fact Connector Chart

Directions: Read the text, record significant facts, and answer the connector questions. When you are finished, answer the questions below the chart in order to reflect on the topic and your skills when completing this activity.

Key topic or concept: _____

Facts	Connector questions
Fact #1	How does fact #1 connect to the key topic or concept?
Fact #2	How are facts #1 and #2 connected to each other?
Fact #3	How is fact #3 connected to facts #1 and #2?

How do these facts help you understand the topic about which you are learning?

_____

_____

What is confusing about identifying the connections among these facts?

_____

_____

Ask Questions

Questioning Squares

Directions: Read the information and record significant facts from the text. Then write questions for three audiences—teacher, author, and classmates.

Key topic or concept: _____

Facts related to the topic:	Questions for the teacher:
Questions for the author:	Questions for the class:

PASSPORT TO COMPREHENSION

Determine Importance

#50469 Successful Strategies

Determine Importance— Main Idea and Supporting Details

The Importance of Identifying the Main Idea

It is essential that students are able to identify the main idea in any text that they encounter. Being able to identify the main idea provides the cognitive foundation for questioning, visualizing, connecting to prior knowledge, and many other sophisticated reading strategies. Some students will be able to identify the main idea quickly by previewing the text. Other students will need to read carefully, examine supporting details, and make a deduction about the main idea. Still other students will struggle with identifying the main idea and need explicit instruction and modeling in order to master this skill. One of the first things you will do in your classroom each year will be diagnosing the students' abilities to identify the main idea. Once you determine students' needs, you will need to use strategies and instructional approaches that meet the diverse needs of all students.

Retelling

The ability to retell is important because it enables students to encapsulate key information as it relates to the main idea. Students need to internalize the following questions in order to master the skill of retelling:

- What is the key concept or main idea in the text?

- What are the important supporting details?

- What is the extraneous information?

- How can I link the important information together?

- How can I relate the information in my own words?

Identifying Theme

The theme, or the "big idea," is what makes the text important and often interesting. However, many students struggle with identifying the theme. An effective way to present the idea of theme is to share a number of common themes with students (good vs. evil, love conquers all, honesty is the best policy, change is inevitable, etc.). Emphasize to students that a theme is a universal idea that helps the reader to understand the world, relationships, or ways of behaving.

Then, have students delve into the text, but guide them toward textual evidence that reveals the theme. Tell students that they will have to look at the text's evidence and make an inference about the theme. In many text selections, particularly in literature, the theme is the main idea. Encourage students to think about the main idea, theme, or key concept whenever they are reading.

Determine Importance— Main Idea and Supporting Details

Finding Evidence to Support the Main Idea

Once students have mastered the skill of identifying the main idea, they need to be accountable for finding evidence that supports the main idea. The following are some tips for helping students find key textual evidence when reading:

1. Reread the text, skimming and scanning for important information.
2. Reread the headings and subheadings to determine supporting evidence.
3. Look at the text features and read the captions.
4. Reread the introduction and conclusion for clues about the supporting details.
5. Work with a partner to discuss and find evidence from the text.
6. Read another text on the same topic and compare supporting details in order to discover what's most important.

Restating Facts and Details

One of the best ways to teach students how to remember and restate facts and details is to have them categorize the information into major subtopics as they read. You will need to begin by giving students explicit instructions on how to organize their notes while they read, or even provide them with a highly structured activity page that requires the students to organize the facts and details into categories. As students gain independence with this skill, you can have them read short portions of text and ask them to identify a category of information and the facts and details that further develop or explain the category. The end goal is to help students become readers who automatically sort and organize information in their minds as they read in order to restate the information in a coherent manner. Achieving this goal requires intense strategy instruction and modeling.

Strategy 1: Previewing for the Main Idea

Text that is highly visual and graphic is very motivating to students. However, it is important that students be able to discern the main idea and supporting details even when previewing, reading, and analyzing graphic texts. Often, students will become distracted by highly graphic texts. They focus on the illustrations, photographs, and charts and fail to come away with an understanding of the main idea of the text. This problem can be solved by providing students with many opportunities to read graphic texts, while making sure to incorporate highly structured previews of the text. Teach students how to identify and retain important information and ignore extraneous information. Use the activity on page 135 to help students learn to use graphic sources. (Standards 5.1, 7.3)

Determine Importance—
Main Idea and Supporting Details

Strategy 2: Concept Wheel

Show students how to fill in the Concept Wheel on page 136. The entire passage's main idea goes in the center circle, and the details from the whole passage that answer the questions radiate from the main idea like spokes on a wheel. (Standards 7.3, 7.5, 7.6)

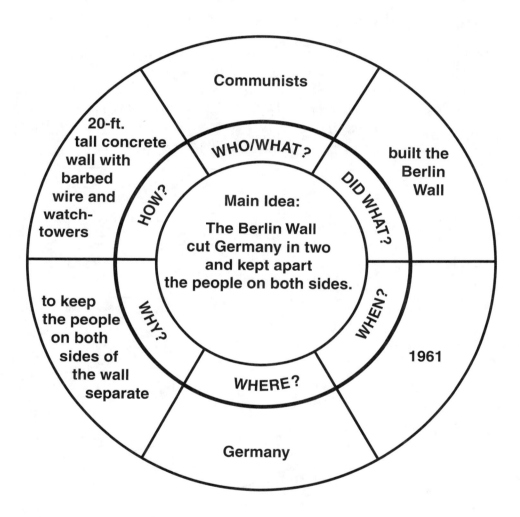

Strategy 3: Artistic Webbing

This strategy is highly motivating to struggling readers because they get to use art to represent the main idea and supporting details. Have them use the Artistic Webbing activity on page 137 to plan their illustrations and to explain how engaging in this activity helps them to understand the text information better. (Standards 7.3, 7.5, 7.6)

Determine Importance—
Main Idea and Supporting Details

Strategy 4: T-Bar Organizer

You can think of the main idea as a bar balanced on top of a column. The column (details) holds up (supports) the main idea. Without the column, the bar would fall, just as without details, the main idea is merely a statement without any proof. The T-Bar Organizer on page 138 is an effective way to represent this idea. The following passage provides an example for using the T-bar organizer to identify the main idea and supporting details from a nonfiction text. (Standards 7.3, 7.5)

Redwood trees live longer than any other living thing on Earth. Many have already lived more than 2,000 years because almost nothing can kill them. They do not die from disease, parasites, termites, fungi, or even forest fires. Although their bark may burn, the core of the tree will survive and re-grow the bark. If lightning strikes them, they will heal. Those blown down by strong winds send up sprouts from the roots that remain in the ground. If a redwood tree is cut down, its stump will send up saplings.

Main Idea

Redwood trees live thousands of years because almost nothing kills them.

Details

They don't die from:

- disease
- parasites
- termites
- fungi
- forest fires
- lightning
- being blown down
- being cut down

Determine Importance—
Main Idea and Supporting Details

Strategy 5: Pyramid Graphic Organizer

Just as a main idea is supported by facts, the top block of a pyramid is supported by the blocks beneath it. Help students to represent graphically the main idea and the supporting details by using the Pyramid Graphic Organizer on page 139. (Standards 7.3, 7.5)

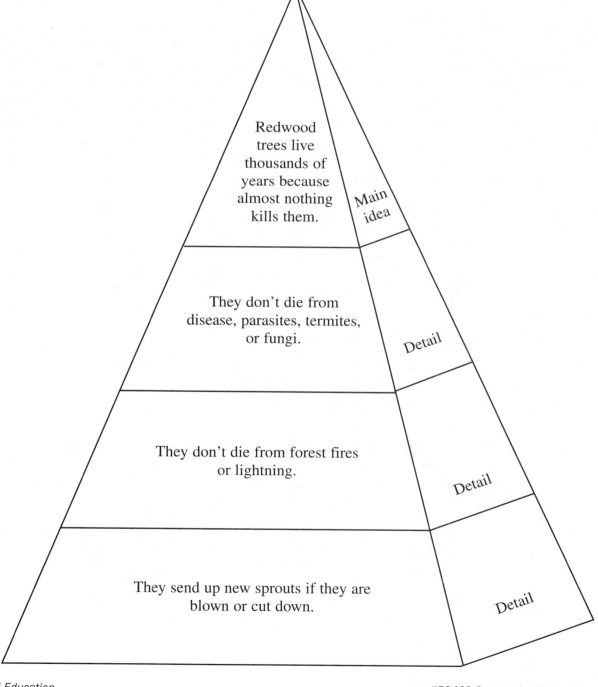

Determine Importance— Main Idea and Supporting Details

Strategy 6: Selecting Important Details

It is important for students to recognize the difference between essential and nonessential details. With practice, students can determine what information is actually important and what is not. Students can do this by choosing the main idea from a passage and selecting the three most important details that support that main idea. Use the activity on page 140 to practice this strategy. (Standards 7.5, 7.6)

Strategy 7: Cognitive Maps

Many different types of mapping strategies can be used to improve students' abilities to find the main idea and supporting details. Cognitive maps can be used with a chapter, a newspaper article, or a description. Cognitive maps can be created by individual students, small groups, or an entire class.

One advantage of using a web or other cognitive map is that students can readily see whether their main idea and supporting details match. After constructing a map, students should check to see that each of the supporting details they have chosen does, in fact, support the main idea they have selected. If not, students should adjust the wording of the main idea so that it accurately fits the information they have read, or they may need to go back and reread the details.

When reading longer works of nonfiction, students can map appropriate sections of text, and then keep their cognitive maps to refresh their memories in preparation for quizzes or tests. In addition, cognitive maps can be used to (Abbott 1999):

- introduce a concept
- connect a concept to a student's frame of reference
- make meaning from text
- review unit concepts
- study words
- teach each other

The types of maps are described below, along with suggestions for their use. Examples of these maps are included on pages 141–144. Reproduce and distribute these organizers anytime students are reading material that lends itself to mapping. Leave additional copies of cognitive maps in a center so that students can help themselves and learn to use them independently. (Standards 5.8, 7.3, 7.5, 7.7)

Star Maps and Webbing: These simple maps allow students to record the main idea in the central part of the map. The spokes and points emanating from the center of the web or star allow space for the students to write supporting details. This type of map is best used when the material is straightforward on a single topic. See page 141 for an example of each map.

Determine Importance— Main Idea and Supporting Details

Strategy 7: Cognitive Maps *(cont.)*

Charts and Matrices: Charts and matrices are used to list attributes and to compare and contrast. For example, students might construct a chart to show the similarities and/or differences between British and Patriot troops during the American Revolution. Charting such information clarifies and organizes it so that students can restate the main idea more simply. See page 142.

Tree Maps: This type of organizer can show classifications, structures, attributes, causal information, and examples. A tree map might be used, for instance, to show the classification of insects. It might also be used to show how one event triggered another, which triggered additional events. See page 143.

Chain Maps: A chain map can show processes, sequences, cause and effect, and chronology. Such a map can be used to follow an election or demonstrate how complex events occur, e.g., poverty or substance abuse. See page 144 for examples of chain maps.

Sketches: Sketches can be used to show physical structures, descriptions of places, spatial relationships, and visual images. A sketch of an animal's habitat, for example, can show how the animal interacts with the various elements within it. Students can draw conclusions about a main idea from looking at a sketch or from constructing one.

Strategy 8: SQ3R

Survey, question, read, recite, and review (SQ3R) (Robinson 1970, as described in Irvin 1998) is an excellent strategy for helping students determine the main idea. Begin by having students survey the text for organizational structure. Research has shown that when students have a strong and accurate awareness of structure, they are better able to determine and retain main ideas and supporting details. Next, have students convert subheadings into questions and find answers as they read. For example, the following subheadings might be found in a passage on frogs and toads and, when turned into questions, could assist students in establishing the main idea and supporting details of the text.

Examples of Subheadings	Converted Into Questions
Similarities Between Frogs and Toads	What are the similarities between frogs and toads?
Each Creature Has Interesting Features!	What are their features?
Fascinating Habitats	What are the habitats of frogs and toads?
Yum-Yum—What They Eat	What do frogs and toads eat?

Divide students into pairs and have them recite a summary or paraphrase of the important information they read by referring to the answers that they generated. In the review stage, students can use graphic organizers to reformulate their knowledge for a deeper understanding. Use pages 145 and 146 with this strategy. (Standards 5.1, 7.3, 7.5)

Determine Importance—Main Idea and Supporting Details

Strategy 9: Identifying Text Patterns

Recognizing the structure of the text can help students better understand nonfiction. There are four main types of text patterns: describing, cause and effect, compare and contrast, and chronological order.

Describing Pattern: A describing pattern often occurs in a text about a singular topic, such as sharks or birds. In this type of work, the student encounters descriptions as well as lists of attributes. For example, a book on sharks might tell about scientific research on sharks or describe the differences among types. This pattern is very common.

Cause-and-Effect Pattern: A cause-and-effect pattern is found in many nonfiction texts that describe scientific processes, such as the formation of rocks. Cause-and-effect patterns discuss outcomes and the reasons they occurred. It answers questions that a reader may have about a topic.

Compare-and-Contrast Pattern: A compare-and-contrast pattern shows the similarities and differences between topics, events, or people. For example, a book may explain how butterflies differ from moths. This pattern may also be used with complicated subjects, like comparing and contrasting cultures or religions.

Chronological Pattern: Chronological patterns discuss events in the order in which they occur or detail the steps in a process. Books about historical periods or instruction manuals are generally written in chronological patterns. Development and change also use a chronological pattern.

Certain words can signal the reader about the type of text pattern. Examples of the signal words that students may encounter in the four types of text are shown below. Students can add to the list as they read across the content areas. (Standards 5.1, 7.7)

Text Pattern	Signal Words
Describing	for example, for instance, as you can see, notice that, specifically
Cause and Effect	as a result, occurs when, therefore, happens when
Compare and Contrast	like, unlike, different from, similar to
Chronological	first, second, last, additionally

Activity sheets to practice identifying patterns are on pages 147 and 148.

Determine Importance—
Main Idea and Supporting Details

Previewing for the Main Idea

Directions: Use the following activity page to preview the text in order to figure out the main idea.

Chapter or section title: _____

Headings and subheadings: _____

Graphic features (Identify and describe):

Identify	Describe
1.	
2.	
3.	

Based on your previewing, what is the main idea? Describe the main idea in your own words.

_____

_____

_____

How did previewing help you to identify the main idea?

_____

_____

_____

Determine Importance—
Main Idea and Supporting Details

Concept Wheel

Directions: Write the main idea of the text in the center. Then fill in the details by answering the questions.

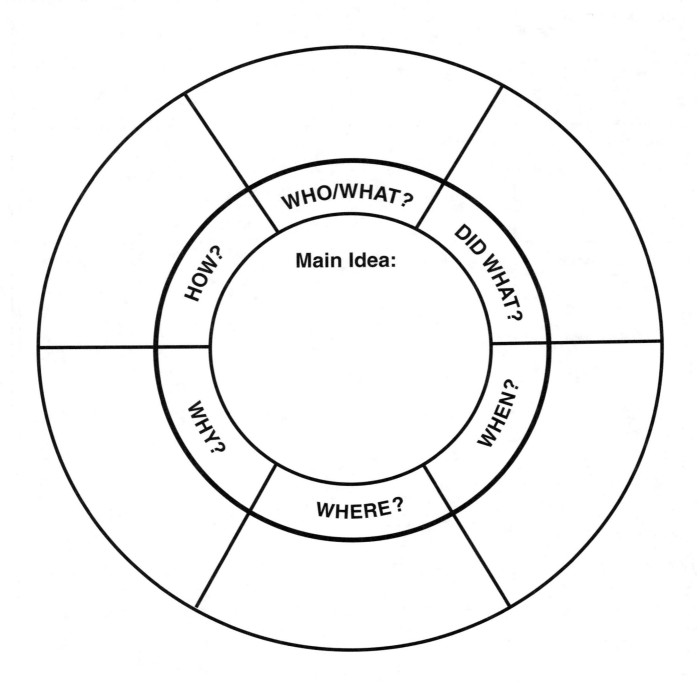

Determine Importance—
Main Idea and Supporting Details

Artistic Webbing

Directions: Use the following "box" web to illustrate the main idea.

Supporting detail:	Supporting detail:
Main idea:	
Supporting detail:	Supporting detail:

How does illustrating the main idea and supporting details help you to understand the information better?

_____

_____

_____

_____

Determine Importance—
Main Idea and Supporting Details

T-Bar Organizer

Directions: Write the main idea in the top box. Then list details to support the main idea.

Main idea:

Details:

Determine Importance—
Main Idea and Supporting Details

Pyramid Graphic Organizer

Directions: Write the main idea in the top of the pyramid. Then fill in details to support the main idea.

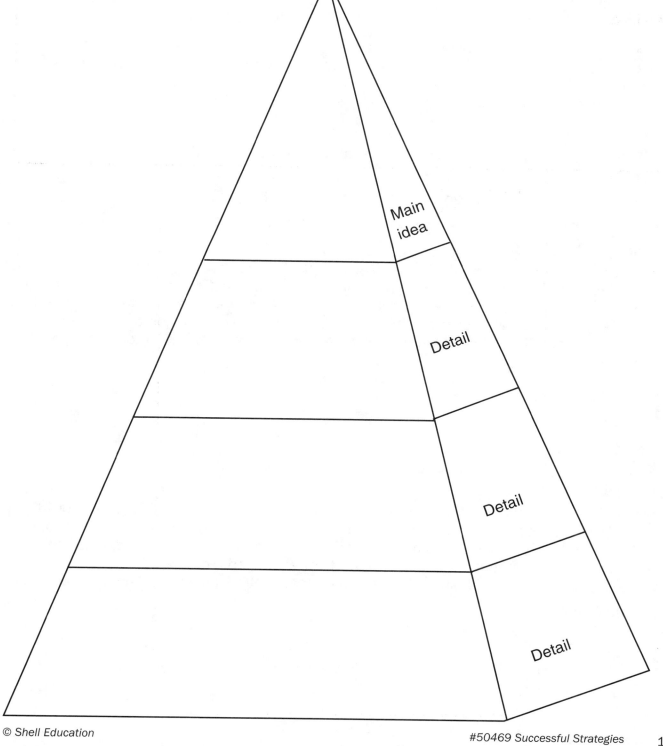

Determine Importance—
Main Idea and Supporting Details

Selecting Important Details

Directions: As you read, it is important to think about which details are essential and which are not. Read the paragraphs below. Then, write the three most important details in each one. An example is given to help you.

American Indian Storytellers

Native North Americans did not have written language before contact with Europeans. Therefore, American Indian tribes depended on storytelling for teaching and discipline. Often, storytellers were chosen at a young age. Only children who memorized the stories quickly and accurately were considered for this respected position.

Important Details:

1. Before Europeans settled in North America, American Indians didn't have written language.

2. American Indians used storytelling instead of written language.

3. Children with good memories were chosen to become storytellers.

American Indian Traders

When modern Americans shop for items, they usually do not know the person who made them. By contrast, Americans Indians knew the source of all the food, clothing, and materials they acquired. Also, everyone appreciated the amount of labor and care that was required to create a woven blanket, a ceramic pot, or a painted buffalo robe. Trade and barter were common practices. Trade fairs were a time when many tribes could gather to exchange goods as well as enjoy dances and feasts.

Important Details:

1. _____

2. _____

3. _____

American Indian Innovations

American Indians developed many types of technologies that made their lives easier or more productive. These included weapons, knives and skinning/tanning implements, looms, cooking utensils, mobile homes, astronomical aids, etc. These varied from region to region. There was more development in regions where the people had more free time, such as Mesoamerica, the Southwest, and the Inca culture that stretched along the Andes Mountains.

Important Details:

1. _____

2. _____

3. _____

Determine Importance—
Main Idea and Supporting Details

Cognitive Maps—Star Maps and Webbing

Star Map

Directions: Use the star map below to record the main idea and supporting details of the assigned passage. Then, on the back of this page or on a separate piece of paper, write a sentence or two that clearly states the main idea.

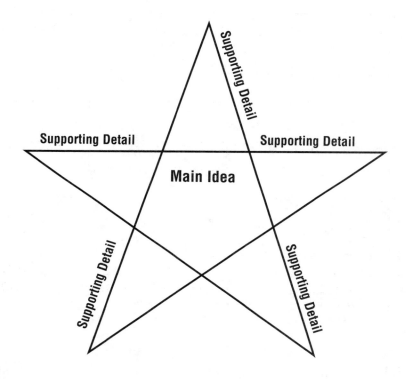

Webbing

Directions: Use the spider map below to record the main idea and supporting details of the assigned passage. Then, on the back of this page or on a separate piece of paper, write a sentence or two that clearly states the main idea.

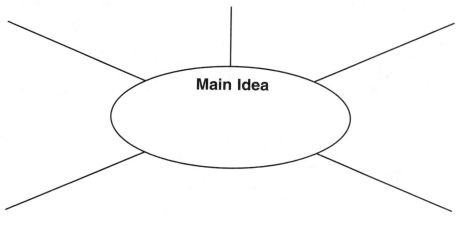

Determine Importance—Main Idea and Supporting Details

Cognitive Maps—Charts and Matrices

Compare-and-Contrast Matrix

Directions: Use the chart below to record information about two groups of people, places, or things that are being compared and contrasted. When you are done, use the back of this page or a separate piece of paper to write a sentence or two that summarizes the main idea.

Attribute	_____ Item 1	_____ Item 2
_____ **Attribute 1**	_____ _____ _____	_____ _____ _____
_____ **Attribute 2**	_____ _____ _____	_____ _____ _____
_____ **Attribute 3**	_____ _____ _____	_____ _____ _____

Venn Diagram

Directions: Write information that two items share in the area where the circles intersect. Write information that is unique to the items in the areas outside the intersection.

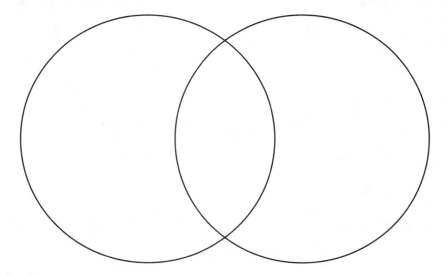

Determine Importance—
Main Idea and Supporting Details

Cognitive Maps—Tree Maps

Network Tree

Directions: Use the tree map below to organize your thoughts about the main idea and supporting details of the assigned passage. When you are finished, use the back of this page or a separate piece of paper to write a sentence or two that clearly states the main idea.

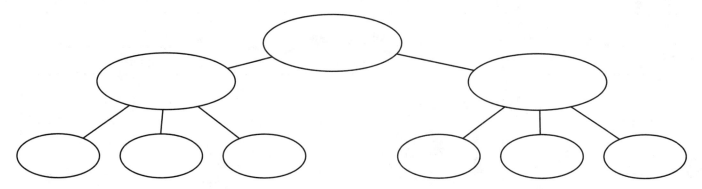

Mind Map

Directions: Use the mind map below to organize your thoughts about the main idea and supporting details of the assigned passage. When you are finished, use the back of this page or a separate piece of paper to write a sentence or two that clearly states the main idea.

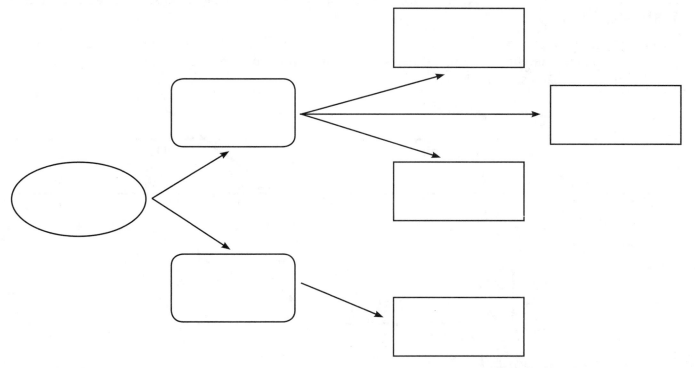

Determine Importance—
Main Idea and Supporting Details

Cognitive Maps—Chain Maps

Cycle Map

Directions: Use the map below to organize information about an event that occurs repeatedly. Once you have organized the cycle, write a sentence or two that clearly describes the main idea on the back of this page or on a separate piece of paper.

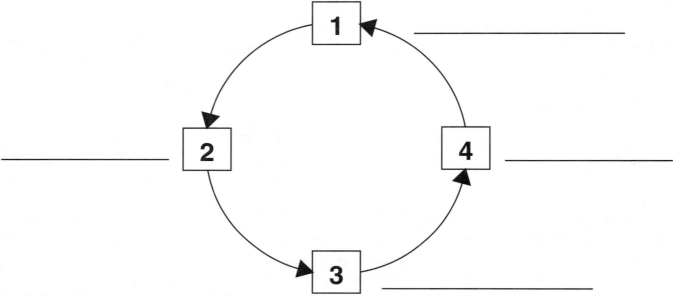

Fishbone Map

Directions: Use the map below to organize information that describes how an event occurred. Once you have organized the information, write a sentence or two that clearly describes the main idea on the back of this page or on a separate piece of paper.

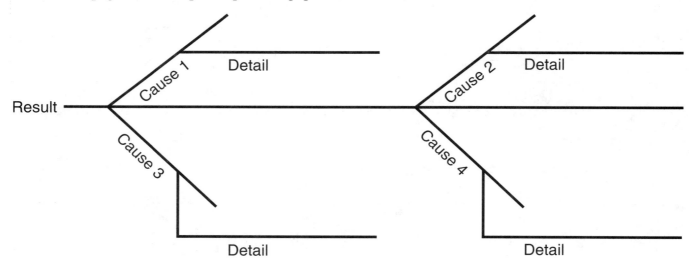

Determine Importance—
Main Idea and Supporting Details

SQ3R—Part 1

Directions: Use the following activity page to identify the main idea and supporting details. Make sure to evaluate the importance of the supporting details.

Concept or topic being studied: _____

Title of the text: _____

Main idea: _____

Directions: Identify supporting details and then rate their importance in understanding the main idea.

1 = Very Important

2 = Somewhat Important

3 = Not Very Important

Supporting Details:	Importance rating:
1.	
2.	
3.	

Do the supporting details help you to better understand the concept that you are studying? Explain.

_____

_____

_____

Determine Importance—
Main Idea and Supporting Details

SQ3R—Part 2

Directions: Answer the following questions to determine the main idea.

What are the text length and structure?	What are the important headings and subheadings?
What should I be sure to read, and in what order should I read it?	What parts of the text should I read very carefully?
What parts of the text do not look important? What should I skip or ignore?	How will the text connect to my prior knowledge?

What is the main idea? _____

How do I know? _____

_____

_____

Determine Importance—
Main Idea and Supporting Details

Identifying Text Patterns

Directions: Read the paragraphs below. Identify which of the four patterns (describing, cause and effect, compare and contrast, and chronological) is suggested by each paragraph. Underline any signal words that you find in the text. Then give the paragraph an appropriate title.

Title: _____

Anyone who has stood on the shore of an ocean and looked out towards the horizon has probably wondered just how big the ocean really is. Specifically, the ocean is a whole, continuous body of salt water covering almost three-quarters (140 million square miles [362.6 million square kilometers] or about 70%) of the earth's surface. It is made up of four oceans: the Pacific, the Atlantic, the Arctic, and the Indian, as well as many smaller seas such as the Mediterranean Sea. These seas and oceans together account for 97% of the earth's water.

Text type: _____

Title: _____

Anyone who has even licked his or her lips after an ocean swim knows that the ocean is salty. But did you know that the salt in the ocean actually comes from the land? The oceans are the source of rainfall for the earth. As water is evaporated from the ocean and turns to rain, the land is weathered. The land becomes sediment that is carried by rivers and, as a result, is returned back into the ocean. Sediments from the rivers, like sodium chloride and potassium sulfate, dissolve in the ocean water to make it salty.

Text type: _____

Determine Importance—
Main Idea and Supporting Details

Identifying Text Patterns *(cont.)*

Title: _____

There are 20,000 species of fish in the oceans, yet only about 300 are caught commercially for food. There are two main types of fish that humans catch for food. Pelagic fish live near the surface of the ocean. Examples include salmon, tuna, and herring. By contrast, demersal fish live on the sea bottom and include such types as flounder and cod. Lobster and crab are also considered to be demersal organisms.

Text type: _____

Title: _____

Leonardo da Vinci designed the first underwater breathing apparatus in the sixteenth century. Three centuries would pass before the bathysphere was created in the 1930s. This device used compressed air within the diving bell and allowed divers greater time under water, which in turn allowed them to explore in greater depths. The forerunner of modern scuba gear was developed by Jacque-Yves Cousteau in the 1940s. In the past 60 years, this technology has improved and become a commonplace item for professional and amateur explorers. The bathysphere has also evolved into the modern-day submarine that allows scientists to explore the ocean floor itself.

Text type: _____

Extension: Examine a passage of nonfiction writing and determine its structure. Then write your own paragraph on a similar topic using the same structure. Include signal words in your paragraph so that your reader will be able to identify the structure you have used. Exchange papers with a classmate and have him or her determine the text type.

Determine Importance—
Text Structures

Introduction

In reading, structure means the way that ideas are organized and presented to the reader. Well-written text will reflect unity and coherence because the ideas will be organized, and the relationships between and among ideas will be made clear to the reader. However, students often encounter "inconsiderate" text in which the ideas are not presented clearly and the relationships between or among ideas are vague, disorganized, or nonexistent. If students have knowledge of structural patterns, they will be able to make sense of well-written text easily. In addition, if students encounter "inconsiderate" text, they will know why the information seems inaccessible and be able to analyze the author by using their knowledge of structural patterns.

Chronological, Logical, and Sequential Order

Texts that are written in sequential order typically show a sequence of steps, ideas, or events. Often, sequential text in social studies will tell the story of a battle, the life of a historical figure, or the forming of a new nation. Sequential text in science will outline the steps of an experiment. In math, sequential text will describe the steps of a particular problem-solving process. Make sure to model for students how to identify sequential order and how to apply this structural approach to their own writing.

Compare and Contrast

Compare-and-contrast texts intend to show the similarities and differences between or among various topics or ideas. For example, a piece of social studies text may delineate the similarities and differences between Greek and Roman myths or among fascist, democratic, socialist, and communist forms of government. A science text may compare various animals that live in the same habitat or the effect of the same chemical compound in different lab experiments. A math text may compare different ways to solve a particular kind of problem. The compare-and-contrast method may involve an element of analysis because the writer may include an evaluation of which method, approach, or idea is the best. However, often the reader is expected to make connections and evaluate the different approaches or ideas by relying on prior knowledge and analytical skills.

Cause and Effect

Text that is organized in a cause-and-effect structure presents the reader with events and the consequences of those events. Often there is a discernable if/then pattern that the reader will be able to recognize. It is important to teach students that even though causes have related effects, there is often a slightly more complicated element to this structure in which the effects are often the "cause" of a new problem that has a new "effect." This particular structure is a chain reaction of events. For example, in the description of a military battle, the enemy may attack the fort, which results in a huge fire. The fire may cause the loss of many lives and ultimately lead to the defeat of those defending the fort. Cause-and-effect structures show readers the relationship between ideas and events. Critical readers should be taught how to assess when a writer is making illogical leaps and attempting to assign a cause-and-effect relationship without adequate support.

Determine Importance— Text Structures

Proposition and Support

When texts are arranged in a proposition-and-support structure, the writer proposes an idea and offers support for the idea. For example, the writer may propose a neighborhood cleanup. Support for this idea may include the following: 1) A neighborhood cleanup will get the community involved and interacting with each other in a positive way. 2) More people working together will help the job get done quickly. 3) If one community cleans up its neighborhood, maybe other communities will follow its example. 4) Setting a good example will ultimately make for a cleaner Earth. The proposition-and-support structure is great for persuasive pieces of writing, including editorials.

Problem and Solution

When writers use problem-and-solution structures, they often will begin by presenting a problem and possible solutions to the problem. Writers may include the pros and cons for the solution. This approach relies heavily on persuasive techniques because the writer often has a particular solution in mind and will craft the text to prove his or her solution. Critical readers need to be taught how to recognize bias and how to evaluate whether or not an argument is balanced.

Progression of Ideas

When writers use progression-of-ideas structures, they list key features about the topic and elaborate on each one. For example, a social studies text may list various features of a geographic region such as India or Saudi Arabia. These features may include government, religion, currency, economy, language, etc. A science text may list various characteristics of a particular species. Readers need to become aware of the pattern of texts written in a progression of ideas format: feature, details; feature, details; feature, details. Often this pattern is offset by headings and subheadings. As readers gain proficiency with text structure, they will learn the author's purpose connected with each structure. Progression of ideas is intended to teach the reader about the topic.

Using Strategies Independently

You will need to identify many different types of text and model for students how to determine text structure, author's purpose, and the reasons that authors choose particular structures to achieve their purposes. When analyzing text structure, you will find that it will not always be clear which structure the author chose to use because he or she may be using a combination of two or more different structures. Share with students your confusions and questions so that they recognize how potentially challenging the identification of text structure can be.

Strategy 1: Text Structures Reference Sheet

Introduce structural patterns to students by showing them examples of the different patterns that authors use when presenting nonfiction information. Duplicate page 156 for students to keep for reference. Use the same handout as a guide for creating charts or posters that can be displayed in the classroom for quick reference. Locate examples in their textbooks that illustrate the different patterns. Encourage students to use their handouts to assist them in identifying and understanding the patterns. (Standards 7.5, 7.7)

Determine Importance— Text Structures

Strategy 2: Flow Charts and Time Lines

These graphic organizers help students to show sequence in a process or a series of events. The same basic process is required—placing one thing or idea after another according to the order in which they occurred. Sequence or flow charts are often used when describing scientific and health processes, such as the stages of human growth and the food chain. Time lines can be used to connect specific dates with events, as in social studies. Templates are on pages 157–159. (Standard 7.7)

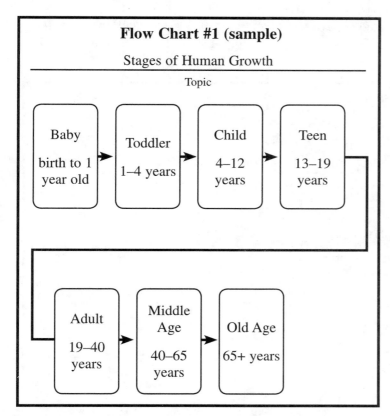

Flow Chart #1 (sample)

Stages of Human Growth
Topic

Baby — birth to 1 year old → Toddler 1–4 years → Child 4–12 years → Teen 13–19 years → Adult 19–40 years → Middle Age 40–65 years → Old Age 65+ years

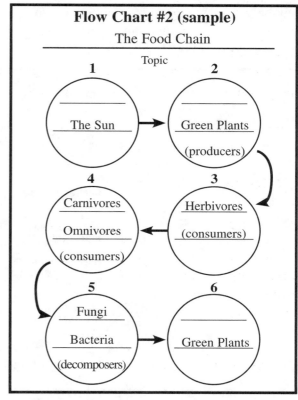

Flow Chart #2 (sample)

The Food Chain
Topic

1 The Sun → 2 Green Plants (producers) → 3 Herbivores (consumers) → 4 Carnivores Omnivores (consumers) → 5 Fungi Bacteria (decomposers) → 6 Green Plants

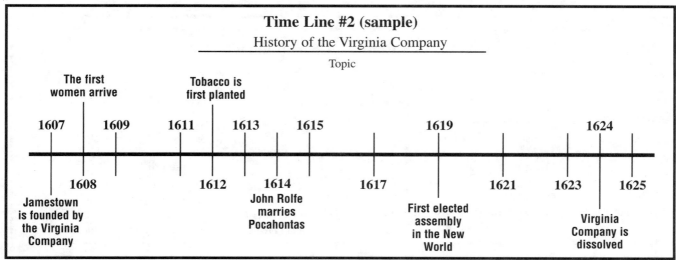

Time Line #2 (sample)

History of the Virginia Company
Topic

1607 · 1608 Jamestown is founded by the Virginia Company · The first women arrive · 1609 · 1611 · 1612 · Tobacco is first planted · 1613 · 1614 John Rolfe marries Pocahontas · 1615 · 1617 · 1619 First elected assembly in the New World · 1621 · 1623 · 1624 Virginia Company is dissolved · 1625

Determine Importance—
Text Structures

Strategy 3: The Venn Diagram and the Compare/Contrast Chart

The charts can be used to illustrate visually and/or organize the similarities and differences between topics, events, or people. To use a Venn diagram, students list unique characteristics of two ideas, things, or events (one in the outside section of the left circle and one in the outside section of the right circle). In the middle section where the circles overlap, students list characteristics that the two have in common. A compare/contrast chart takes two ideas, things, or events and requires students to state in more precise terms how they are alike and different. The benefits for using either organizer are that they help students arrange knowledge and ideas in a specified order. These are also excellent prewriting strategies to use when summarizing information. Templates are on pages 160 and 161. (Standard 7.7)

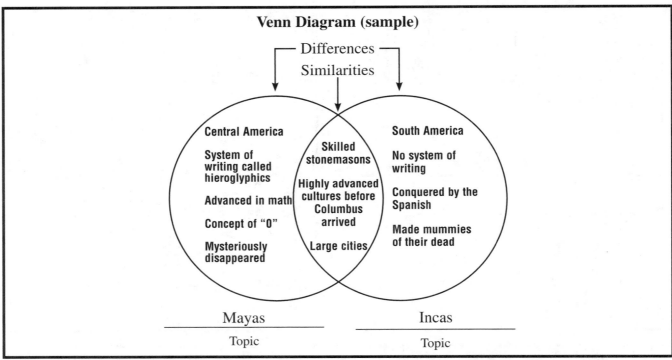

Venn Diagram (sample)

Differences

Similarities

Central America
- System of writing called hieroglyphics
- Advanced in math
- Concept of "0"
- Mysteriously disappeared

Skilled stonemasons

Highly advanced cultures before Columbus arrived

Large cities

South America
- No system of writing
- Conquered by the Spanish
- Made mummies of their dead

Mayas — Topic

Incas — Topic

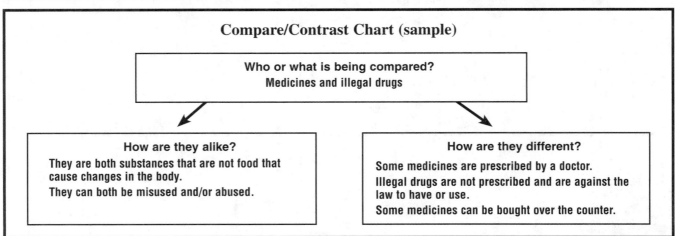

Compare/Contrast Chart (sample)

Who or what is being compared?
Medicines and illegal drugs

How are they alike?
They are both substances that are not food that cause changes in the body.
They can both be misused and/or abused.

How are they different?
Some medicines are prescribed by a doctor.
Illegal drugs are not prescribed and are against the law to have or use.
Some medicines can be bought over the counter.

Determine Importance—
Text Structures

Strategy 4: The Cause/Effect Chart and the Chain of Related Events Organizer

These charts are often used in fictional literature studies, but can be applied in the study of the content areas as well. For example, students can use the Cause/Effect Chart to examine the effects, or consequences, of unhealthy choices. Students seem to grasp the concept of cause and effect more readily when the effect is placed before its cause. The Chain of Related Events organizer is a great visual for understanding historical events and how one event causes another event, which then causes another, which causes another, and so on. Blank charts are on pages 162 and 163. (Standard 7.7)

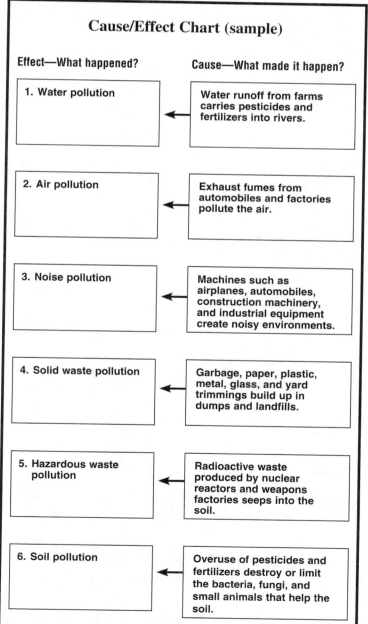

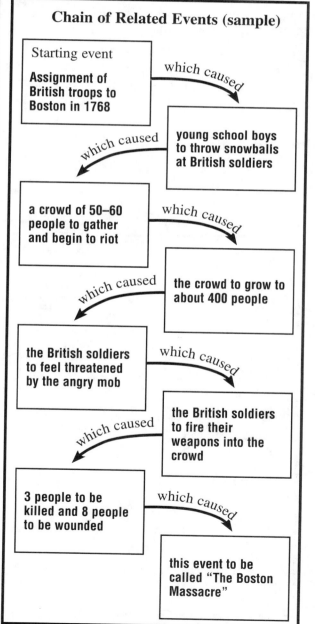

Determine Importance—
Text Structures

Strategy 5: The One Problem/Many Choices Chart and the Decision Tree

Closely related to the cause/effect organizers, these charts are strategies that students can employ to illustrate real or possible outcomes or different actions. These charts can give structure to the decision-making process. Blank charts are on pages 164 and 165. (Standards 7.6, 7.7)

(*Note: It is important to have students realize that their decision for choosing a particular solution is very individual and based on personal beliefs and values. Therefore, no solution has been offered in the sample here.)

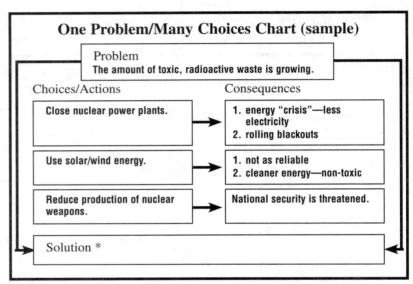

One Problem/Many Choices Chart (sample)

Problem
The amount of toxic, radioactive waste is growing.

Choices/Actions — Consequences

Close nuclear power plants. → 1. energy "crisis"—less electricity 2. rolling blackouts

Use solar/wind energy. → 1. not as reliable 2. cleaner energy—non-toxic

Reduce production of nuclear weapons. → National security is threatened.

Solution *

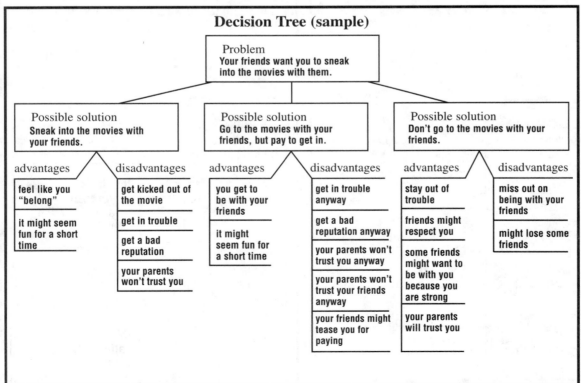

Decision Tree (sample)

Problem
Your friends want you to sneak into the movies with them.

Possible solution
Sneak into the movies with your friends.

Possible solution
Go to the movies with your friends, but pay to get in.

Possible solution
Don't go to the movies with your friends.

advantages
feel like you "belong"

it might seem fun for a short time

disadvantages
get kicked out of the movie

get in trouble

get a bad reputation

your parents won't trust you

advantages
you get to be with your friends

it might seem fun for a short time

disadvantages
get in trouble anyway

get a bad reputation anyway

your parents won't trust you anyway

your parents won't trust your friends anyway

your friends might tease you for paying

advantages
stay out of trouble

friends might respect you

some friends might want to be with you because you are strong

your parents will trust you

disadvantages
miss out on being with your friends

might lose some friends

Determine Importance— Text Structures

Strategy 6: Problem/Solution Organizer and Service Learning

Identify the many ways that students could positively impact their school or neighborhood communities. Provide them with the Problem/Solution Organizer activity on page 166. Tell the students that they need to plan a project in which they identify a real audience, identify a problem that impacts that audience, and brainstorm solutions for the problem. Model for the students by providing text that shows problem and solution structure. Inform students that if they understand persuasive techniques and problem and solution structure, they will be able to provide meaningful service to their communities. Some ideas for this project could be cleaning up litter, planting trees in the community, fixing playground equipment, or painting a mural that reflects the cultural heritage and background of the local citizens. (Standards 7.7, 8.15)

Strategy 7: Narrative Frame

Give students various dramatic topics from different subject areas and provide accompanying texts, if possible (survival of the arctic fox, the Battle of Waterloo, the Watergate scandal, the creation of the hydrogen bomb, etc.). Have students use the Narrative Frame organizer on page 167 to map out the narrative structure of these topics. Point out to the students that even though we associate stories with literature, many real-life events have narrative characteristics. (Standard 7.7)

Strategy 8: Structure Words

Divide students into groups and give them small segments of text in which the structure words have been deleted. Have students refer to the Structure Words activity on page 168 to identify the best words to "sew" the text back together and to help them identify the structure that the author chose to use. The following example demonstrates how useful this activity can be to teach students the significance of structure words in text. (Standard 7.7)

A tree will undergo many changes throughout the year as the seasons change. _____ (*First*), the leaves of a tree turn into brilliant colors in fall. They also begin to fall off the tree. _____ (*Then*), winter brings cold weather and tree limbs are bare. Most trees are without any leaves at all. _____ (*Next*), springtime means that buds are growing and trees are beginning to bloom again. _____ (*Finally*), summer months with lots of sunshine mean that trees continue to grow leaves and remain green. This cycle occurs each year!

Determine Importance—
Text Structures

Text Structures Reference Sheet

The authors of your textbooks write in certain ways that will help you to understand the information you are reading. These styles of writing are called structural patterns. You will usually find different kinds of structural patterns used in the same textbook. Learning to recognize these patterns and read their signal words will help you to become a better reader.

Signal words:

additionally	earlier	last	second
another	finally	later	then
before	first	next	

Compare-and-Contrast Pattern

This pattern shows similarities and differences between different ideas. Signal words:

although	different from	likewise	similarly
as well as	however	most	similar to
but	in comparison	on the other hand	unlike
by contrast	instead	opposites	whereas
conversely	like	rather	while
			yet

Cause-and-Effect Patterns

These patterns tell the result of an event and the reasons it happened. Signal words:

as a result	for this reason	on account of	thereby
because	if…then	since	therefore
consequently	leads to	so that	this led to
due to	nevertheless	then…so	thus

Proposition-and-Support Pattern

This pattern presents a theory and offers examples to support it. Signal words:

a reason for	propose	the evidence is
conclude	research shows	

Progression-of-Ideas Pattern

This pattern describes something and then lists the supporting details. Signal words:

for example	in other words
for instance	that is to say

Determine Importance—
Text Structures

Flow Chart #1

Directions: Use this flow chart to show sequence in a process or in a series of events.

Topic _____

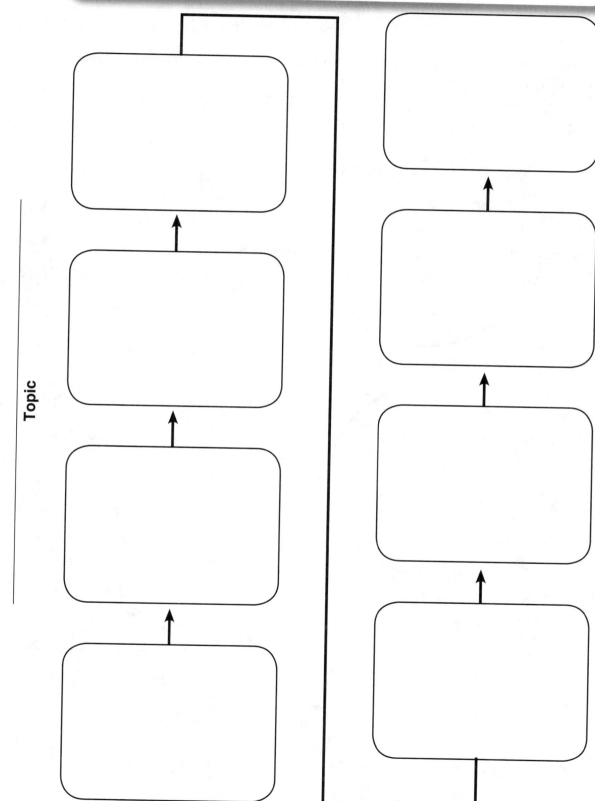

Determine Importance—
Text Structures

Flow Chart #2

Directions: Use this flow chart to show sequence in a process or in a series of events.

Topic

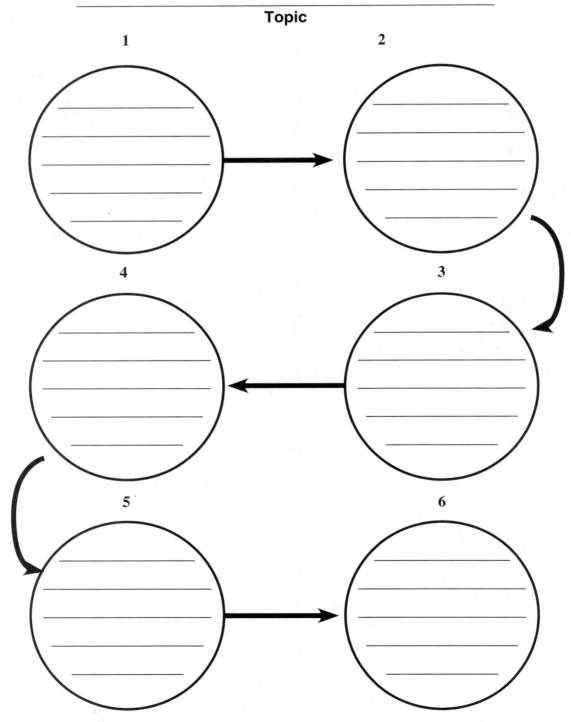

Determine Importance—
Text Structures

Time Line

Directions: Use this time line to show sequence in a series of events.

Topic

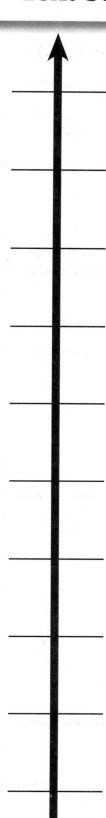

Determine Importance—Text Structures

Venn Diagram

Directions: Use this Venn diagram to compare and/or contrast two topics.

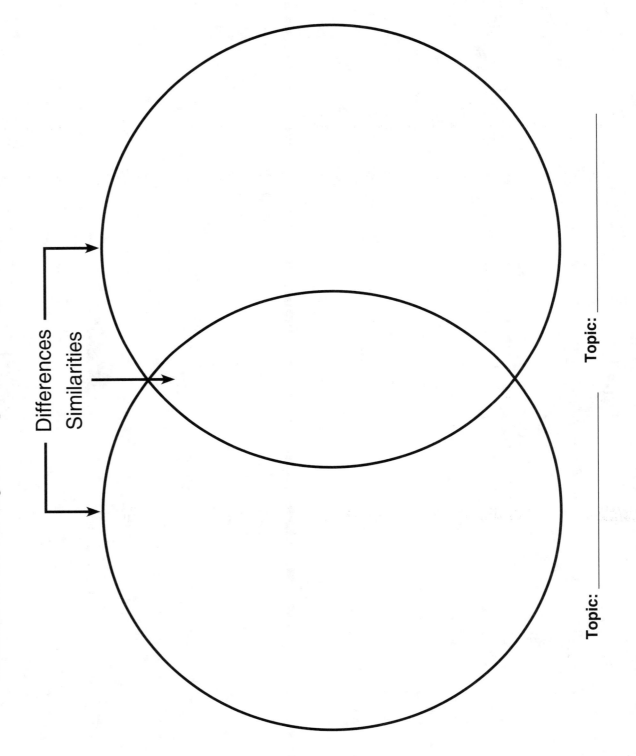

Differences

Similarities

Topic: _____

Topic: _____

Determine Importance—
Text Structures

Compare/Contrast Chart

Directions: Use this chart to compare and/or contrast two topics.

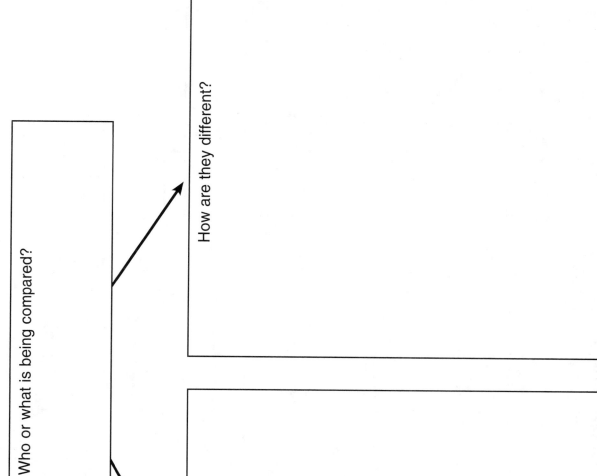

Who or what is being compared?

How are they different?

How are they alike?

Determine Importance— Text Structures

Cause/Effect Chart

Directions: Use this chart to determine the causes and effects of an event.

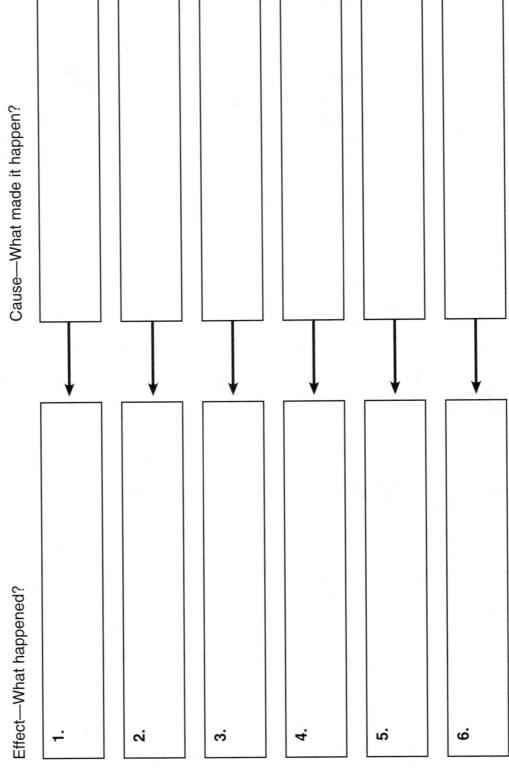

Cause—What made it happen?

Effect—What happened?

1.

2.

3.

4.

5.

6.

Determine Importance—
Text Structures

Chain of Related Events

Directions: Use this chart to determine the causes and effects of an event.

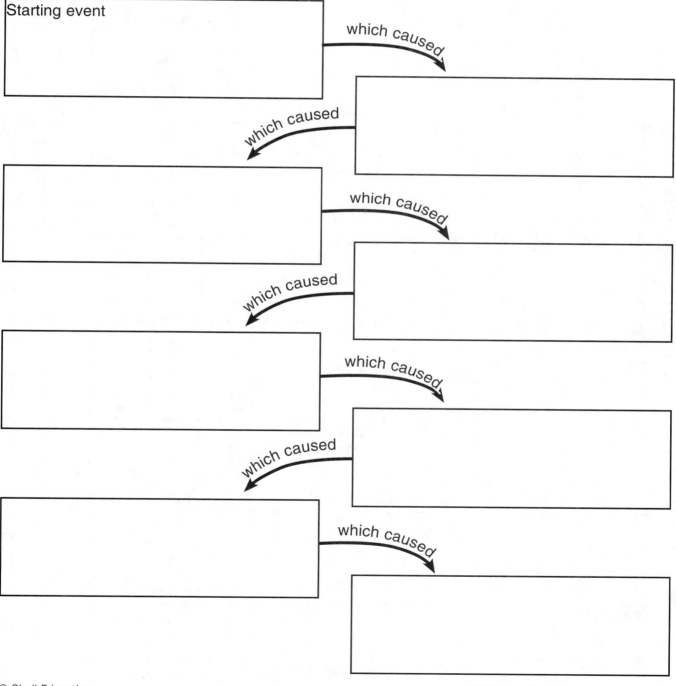

Determine Importance—Text Structures

One Problem/Many Choices Chart

Directions: Use this chart to look at a problem, the actions that could be taken, the consequences of those actions, and then suggest a solution.

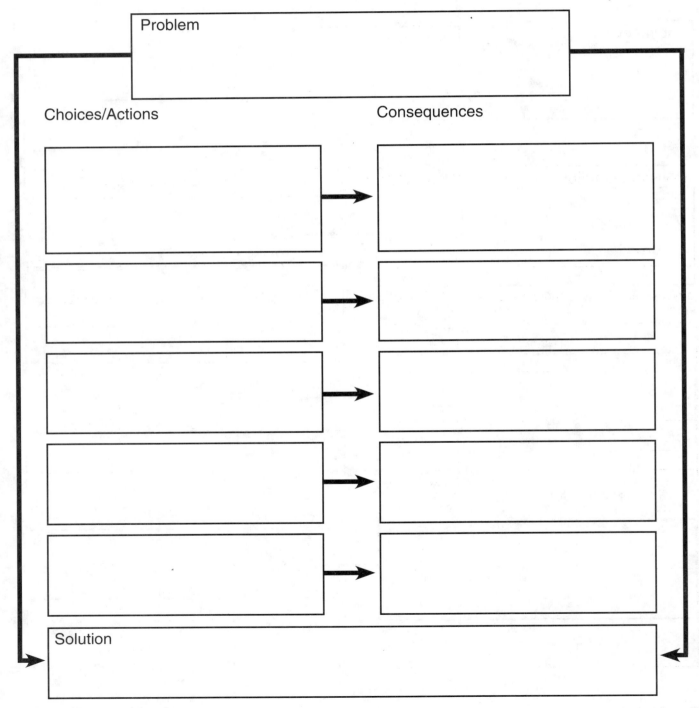

Problem

Choices/Actions

Consequences

Solution

Determine Importance— Text Structures

Decision Tree

Directions: Use this chart to look at a problem, three possible solutions, and the advantages and disadvantages of each solution.

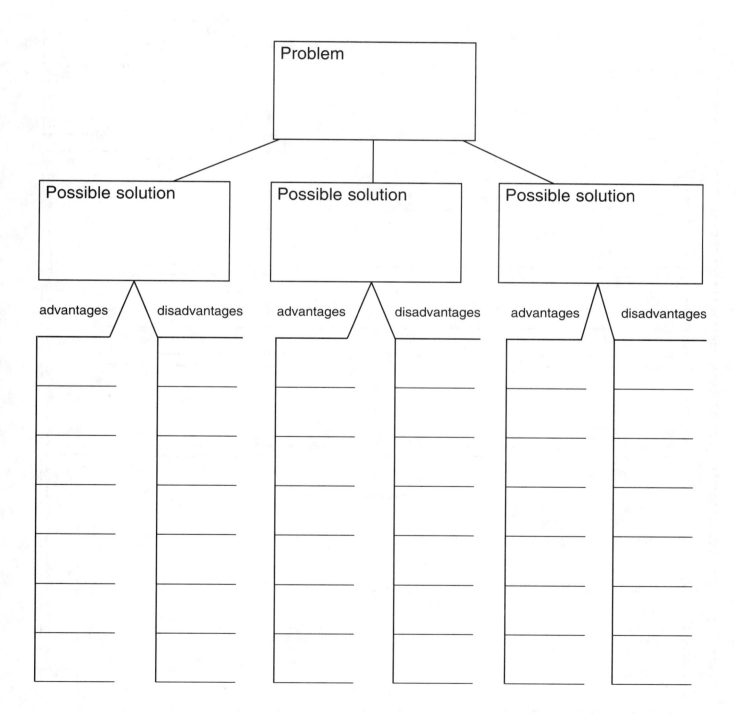

Determine Importance—
Text Structures

Problem/Solution Organizer

Directions: Use the following organizer to identify the problem, solution, pros, and cons described in the text.

Problem:

Solution:

Pros	Cons

Determine Importance—
Text Structures

Narrative Frame

Directions: Use this graphic organizer to identify the narrative elements of a nonfiction piece of text.

People

Place and Time

Event #1:

Event #2:

Event #3:

Conclusion:

Determine Importance—
Text Structures

Structure Words

Directions: Use the following chart to guide you in completing the activity.

Pattern	Structure words
Description or listing	for example, for instance, another, specifically, besides, also, in addition, in particular, particularly, moreover, furthermore
Cause/Effect	consequently, therefore, thus, as a result, however, hence, thereby, leads to, if/then
Compare/Contrast	however, on the other hand, but, by contrast, yet, unlike, like, in comparison, although, whereas, similar to, different from, similarly
Order/Sequence	next, first, last, second, another, then, furthermore, also, additionally, in the first place, in conclusion
Proposition/Support	most importantly, in support, first, next, last, in conclusion
Problem/Solution	unfortunately, first, next, finally, last, in conclusion

1. As you read, copy two sentences that use structure words: _____

   _____

   _____

   _____

   _____

2. What structure is the author using? How do you know? _____

   _____

   _____

   _____

   _____

Determine Importance— Text Organizers

Introduction

Reading is an act of comprehension that requires the reader to construct meaning based on his or her prior knowledge. A higher frequency of reading and writing experiences results in an expansion of students' prior knowledge base. Because reading is not merely phonics or decoding, it is vital to provide students with many opportunities to interact with print. Interacting with print involves self-monitoring, summarizing, and question-generating strategies that students employ to construct meaning. Building students' repertoire of reading strategies enables them to self-monitor and regulate their own reading based on the purpose at hand. Students need to be given daily opportunities to share and discuss what they have read. This sharing helps students to value the reading strategies that they have applied and motivates them to try new ones. In reading content-area materials, students should be offered multiple and varied opportunities to engage in meaningful reading experiences.

Text Organizers

Text organizers are important features in nonfiction texts because they facilitate metacomprehension and help the reader locate information. Publishers of good nonfiction textbooks include many text organizers so that their books may be more easily read and understood by students. Some of these organizers include chapter titles, headings, topics, "alternative" typeface, graphic features, and topic and summary sentences. Learning to recognize and use these text organizers will increase comprehension and foster effective study strategies, such as summarizing and note taking.

Chapter Titles

Chapter titles should provide clear information regarding the main idea of the entire reading selection. Often chapter titles are accompanied by a picture, illustration, photograph, brief explanation, or quote that further expands the information that the author wants the reader to gain. As students are reading the entire selection, they should think about how the headings, subheadings, topic and summary sentences, facts, and details all work together to support and elaborate upon the chapter title.

Using Headings and Subheadings

Headings and subheadings serve to cue the reader about major or minor categories of information. One way to help students utilize headings and subheadings productively is to teach them to read in order to confirm the headings or subheadings. For example, if the heading is "Causes of the American Revolution," students should be encouraged to read to confirm that there were reasons for the American Revolution and that the text will explain those reasons. Emphasize that headings and subheadings add a level of predictability to text that will help them to comprehend more information.

Determine Importance— Text Organizers

Using Typeface

Typeface is a key indicator of important information. Typeface can be large, small, colorful, bold, italicized, squiggly, 3-dimensional, bubbly, cartoon-like, etc. Typeface may reveal importance, but it can also reveal the tone, message, or intent of the text. Teaching students how to evaluate typeface is a critical component to helping them find important information. Some questions that may help students include:

- Describe the typeface. What does it look like?
- What is your immediate reaction to the typeface?
- What do you think the author wants you to think or believe about the topic as a result of reading the typeface?
- How does the typeface reveal important information?
- Is the typeface misleading in any way? Explain.

Using Graphic Features

In today's world we are inundated with text that is heavily laden with graphic features. Magazines, advertisements, and the Internet all boast a huge variety of graphic features designed to shape and sometimes manipulate our understanding of the information. It is critical that we teach students how to evaluate which text features enhance and detract from text information. Some questions that may help students include:

- What are the graphic features in the text?
- How do these graphic features help you to understand the text?
- Are there any graphic features that hinder your understanding? Explain.
- What graphic features are missing? How would the addition of charts, maps, or diagrams aid your understanding of the text?

Examining Topic and Summary Sentences

When students understand that topic and summary sentences reveal the generalizations related to the main idea, they will be able to identify more easily the facts and details that support those generalizations within the heart of the paragraph. Questions to help students make sense of topic and summary sentences include:

- What is the topic sentence?
- How does the topic sentence support the main idea of the entire piece of text?
- What is the summary sentence?
- How does the summary sentence support or connect to the main idea of the entire piece of text?
- What are the facts and details within the paragraph?
- How do these facts and details support the topic sentence?
- How do these facts and details lead to the summary sentence?

Determine Importance—
Text Organizers

Using Strategies Independently

A proficient reader will use text organizers to preview text, to read text comprehensively, and to review information. Make sure to model for students how to use text organizers for each of these purposes. Allow students to work in small groups or with partners to build their proficiency in using text organizers to make meaning of the information. Move toward allowing students to practice these skills independently.

Strategy 1: Text Organizer Scavenger Hunt

Divide students into groups of four. Give them a time limit of five to ten minutes, depending on the maturity and ability of the group and the complexity of the text. Instruct them to get out a blank sheet of paper and identify each text organizer in the chapter and whether or not it connects directly to the chapter title. Reward the first group to finish the scavenger hunt. (Standards 5.1, 7.3)

Strategy 2: Text Organizers Reference Sheet

Duplicate page 175 for students to keep for reference. Use the same handout as a guide for creating charts or posters that can be displayed in the classroom for quick reference. (Standard 7.3)

Strategy 3: Breaks in Text Practice

Headings, subheadings, topics, and summary sentences sum up the important information or main ideas from text. Headings and subheadings help readers find important information or main ideas in text-heavy nonfiction. Print features such as bold or italics may emphasize these breaks in text. Summary sentences will sum up important information, too. It is necessary for a strong reader to notice, read, and understand these breaks in text and to understand how these breaks are related to the meaning of the text. Have students complete the Breaks in Text Practice activity on page 176. This activity can be done as a whole class, in small groups, as partners, or individually, depending on the skill levels in the class. (Standard 7.3)

Strategy 4: Examining Summary Sentences

Have students write paragraphs about the topic or concept they are studying in class. Remind them to include a topic sentence and supporting sentences. Allow students an opportunity to revise their paragraphs for clarity and completeness. Have students switch papers and create a summary sentence for their peer's writing based on the information provided in the paragraph. Students discuss with their partners their reasoning when crafting their summary sentences. After discussion, allow peers to revise their summary sentences as necessary. Remind students that they should not just restate the facts of the paragraph; rather, they should summarize and extend the ideas in the paragraph in a way that is insightful and meaningful. You may have to model how to create the "missing" summary sentence. Use the Examining Summary Sentences activity on page 177 to have students find summary sentences of paragraphs and the important facts and/or details related to the summary sentences. (Standard 7.3)

Determine Importance—
Text Organizers

Strategy 5: Prediction Chart

A strategy that will help students focus on the text, its organization, and its contents is a prediction chart. In the first column of the chart, write in the heading of the chapter that you are examining. In the second column titled "My Prediction," students make predictions based on the title of that heading. Working in a whole-group setting, brainstorm with students a reasonable prediction based on the subject of the textbook, the title of the chapter, and the title of the heading. Record this information on a transparency made from page 178 or on a sheet of butcher or chart paper. As you are recording, be sure to ask students to tell why they would make this prediction. This questioning provides for verification of their prior knowledge, as well as leading the thought processes to other knowledge. The last column titled "What Happened" confirms or disputes the prediction. This chart can be modified for use in a variety of settings, such as watching a video, performing a lab experiment, attending a field trip, or listening to a guest speaker. When using this strategy in a variety of settings, students will begin to realize the connection between reading for information and building their knowledge through alternate resources. (Standards 5.3, 7.7)

Prediction Chart (sample)

Chapter Title: Protection Against Disease

Heading title	My prediction	What happened
What types of microbes are there?	It's going to tell me what microbes cause what diseases.	Viruses cause colds, chicken pox, measles, and rabies. Bacteria cause strep throat and food poisoning. Fungi cause athlete's foot and ringworm.
How do microbes spread?	It's going to tell me how people can get these diseases.	Contaminated water Spoiled or contaminated food Insects and animals

Determine Importance— Text Organizers

Strategy 6: Looking at Chapter Titles

Provide students with a copy of a selection of text in which the title has been deleted. Using the activity on page 179, have them read the text information carefully, noting headings, subheadings, and graphic features. Discuss with the class possible chapter or text titles and have them vote on the one that seems to best represent the information in the text. Reveal to students the title that the author chose and ask students to determine which title best suits the text, theirs or the author's. Ask them to provide ample justification for their selection either orally or in writing. (Standard 7.3)

Strategy 7: Bold and Italicized Words

Inform students that important words are bold or italicized in certain kinds of text. These words are usually key terms with definitions that are critical in fully comprehending the text. You may want to call these key words the "golden" words of the text. Provide students with text in which important words are not bold or italicized and challenge them to underline, circle, or highlight the golden words. They can complete the task independently, and then share their text with a partner, discussing whether or not each partner selected the same words. As a variation, students write expository text about a given topic and write the "golden" key words on a separate sheet of paper. Instruct students to switch papers with a peer and have their peer identify the key words. Students then discuss their selections with a brief justification as a conclusion to the activity. Use the activity on page 180 for practice with this strategy. (Standard 7.3)

Strategy 8: Graphic Features

Students should use the graphic organizer on page 181 to help them think about how the graphic features in the text that they are reading reveal the main idea and other important information. This is a great activity to do with small groups of students. Students can work together to determine the graphic features in the text and then can think about how these graphic features contribute to the text. Do they help determine the main idea? What important information does the author want the reader to gain from the graphic features? (Standards 5.10, 7.3)

Strategy 9: Determining the Purpose of Text Organizers

It is helpful for students to make a list of the text organizers used in a piece of text—whether it is a chapter, a magazine article, a news story, etc. Students can use the chart on page 182 to make a list of the text organizers that are used and then determine the purpose for each text organizer. Students can also make a list of questions that they have about the organizers. (Standards 7.3, 8.2)

Strategy 10: Converting Headings and Subheadings to Questions

Having students convert headings and subheadings into questions is one way to get them to recognize the importance of these text organizers (page 183). At first, they will need your guidance in making questions. For example, if a heading is "Photosynthesis," some students may not automatically know to create the question, "What is photosynthesis?" The best way to assist students is to remind them of the 5 W's and How and then give them a number of headings and subheadings and have them convert them into questions in a group, with a partner, and then independently. (Standards 7.3, 8.2)

Determine Importance— Text Organizers

Strategy 11: Adding Text Organizers

Provide students with text that does not have any text organizers. Remind students of the different text organizers: headings, subheadings, charts, diagrams, graphs, maps, illustrations, photographs, cartoons, captions, etc. Instruct students to find places in the text where a text organizer would really help them to understand the text better. Use the activity on page 184. Depending on the maturity and ability of the class, invite students to actually create a few of the text organizers for the text. If students decide to create graphs, charts, or diagrams, you may have to take them to the school library to do further research on the topic. (Standard 7.3)

Strategy 12: Buddy Reading

Interacting with peers is an essential component for developing proficiency in reading. Students find group work highly motivating, and when it is structured, you can greatly maximize student learning. Allow the students to work with a partner to complete the Buddy Reading activity on page 185 to identify how one text organizer reveals important information and informs the reader about the main idea in the text. It is imperative that students are continually directed to think about how the content of the text and the text organizers are intended to work together to teach them about the main idea. (Standards 7.3, 7.5)

Strategy 13: Investigating the Internet

Having students evaluate appropriate Web sites and Web pages will help them to transfer their critical reading skills to technology. Make sure you work closely with the computer teacher or the school librarian to ensure that all sites are appropriate for students. Have students examine how the color, size, shape, movement, content, and placement of the text organizers influence their understanding of the text information. (Standard 7.3)

Strategy 14: Comparing Two Texts

Comparing texts is a good way to further extend students' abilities to think critically about text and to evaluate the effectiveness of text organizers. Divide students into partners and provide them with at least two different texts. Distribute the Comparing Two Texts activity on page 186, and have students use the rating system to evaluate the effectiveness of the first piece of text. Have them follow the same procedure for the second piece of text. Encourage students to discuss the effectiveness ratings as they complete the activity page and to provide justification for their thinking in their discussion. Again, have them think about how the color, size, placement, and content of the organizers helps or hinders their understanding of the text information. Finally, have them give an overall effectiveness rating to the texts and decide which author did a better job including text organizers. (Standard 7.3)

Determine Importance— Text Organizers

Text Organizers Reference Sheet

Chapter Titles, Headings, Topics

- Signal information to stop and notice
- Let the reader know what information can be found in the passage

Boldface type

Italics

Color print

Text boxes

Bullets

- Signal importance in text
- "This is important information. Pay close attention."

Graphic Features

➤ **Illustrations**

➤ **Photos**

➤ **Diagrams**

➤ **Maps**

➤ **Tables**

➤ **Graphs**

➤ **Charts**

- Help you visualize information
- Organize information in your mind
- Help you to remember the information you have read

Determine Importance— Text Organizers

Breaks in Text Practice

Directions: Circle the answer that shows the best heading where the listed information would be found.

1. jellybeans, chocolate bunnies, colored eggs, colorful baskets

   a. My Favorite Candy   b. Easter Favorites   c. Around the Farm

2. Abraham Lincoln, Rosa Parks, Martin Luther King, Jr.

   a. Famous Presidents   b. Men in History   c. Freedom Fighters

3. pencils, crayons, glue, chairs, desks

   a. Writing Instruments   b. Student Starts School   c. School District Purchases

Directions: What information would you expect to find under the given heading? Circle your answer.

1. **Title:** The Rain forest   **Heading:** Mammals
   a. toucan, anaconda, jaguar
   b. understory, canopy, emergent layer
   c. jaguar, howler monkey, anteater
   d. butterfly, ant, bat

2. **Title:** The Rain forest   **Heading:** Flying Animals
   a. ant, anaconda, jaguar
   b. understory, canopy, emergent layer
   c. jaguar, howler monkey, anteater
   d. butterfly, toucan, bat

3. **Title:** The Rain forest   **Heading:** Layers of the Rain forest
   a. toucan, anaconda, jaguar
   b. understory, canopy, forest floor
   c. jaguar, ant, anteater
   d. butterfly, ant, bat

Extension: Create three questions like the ones above. Create a heading and three or four groups of information, one of which would be the correct answer. Exchange your questions with a friend and try to answer each other's questions.

Determine Importance—
Text Organizers

Examining Summary Sentences

Directions: Use the following chart to record the summary sentences of paragraphs and the important facts and/or details related to the summary sentences.

Summary sentences	Important facts or details in the paragraph

How do the summary sentences relate to the chapter title or the main idea of the selection?

_____

_____

_____

_____

Which facts or details are most important for you to know? Why do you think so?

_____

_____

_____

_____

_____

Determine Importance—
Text Organizers

Prediction Chart

Chapter Title: _____

Heading title	My prediction	What happened

Determine Importance—
Text Organizers

Looking at Chapter Titles

Directions: Use the following graphic organizer to think about the chapter title and its connection to the main ideas and supporting details of the chapter.

Chapter Title: _____

What does the chapter title reveal about the main idea of the chapter? What do you think will happen?	What does the chapter title reveal about what the author wants you to learn?
What are some of the headings and subheadings in the chapter, and how do they connect to the chapter title?	What questions do you have about the chapter?

Determine Importance— Text Organizers

Bold and Italicized Words

Directions: Use the following activity page to define and determine the importance of bold and/or italicized words.

Bold or italicized word	Definition	Response: Why is this word important? How does it connect to the main idea?

Determine Importance—Text Organizers

Graphic Features

Directions: Use the following graphic organizer to help you think about how the graphic features in the text reveal the main idea and other important information.

Graphic features (illustrations, photographs, captions, charts, graphs, maps, etc.)	Response: How does this graphic feature help you to determine the main idea? What important information does the author want you to learn from this graphic feature?

Determine Importance—
Text Organizers

Determining the Purpose of Text Organizers

Directions: Use the following chart to determine the purpose of the text organizers and any questions you have about the organizers.

Chapter Title: _____

Text organizer	Purpose	Questions

Determine Importance—Text Organizers

Converting Headings and Subheadings to Questions

Directions: Change two of the headings or subheadings in the text into questions, answer the question, and write reactions to the answers.

Heading/Subheading as a question: _____

_____

Answer: _____

_____

_____

_____

_____

Reaction: (How does this relate to my life? What further questions do I have?)

_____

_____

_____

_____

Heading/Subheading as a question: _____

_____

Answer: _____

_____

_____

_____

_____

Reaction: (How does this relate to my life? What further questions do I have?)

_____

_____

_____

_____

Determine Importance—
Text Organizers

Adding Text Organizers

Directions: Read a nonfiction text that does not have any text organizers. Find the important information and record it in the left column of the chart. Then think of a text organizer that would enhance the text and describe or illustrate your idea.

Important text information	Your idea for a text organizer

Determine Importance—
Text Organizers

Buddy Reading

Directions: With a partner, use the following activity page to determine how text organizers reveal important information or the main idea in the text.

Buddy #1: Identify and describe a text organizer.	Buddy #1: Does the text organizer reveal important information? Explain.
Buddy #2: Identify and describe a text organizer.	Buddy #2: Does the text organizer tell you more about the main idea in the text? Explain.

Determine Importance— Text Organizers

Comparing Two Texts

Directions: Use the following chart to compare the text organizers in two different pieces of text.

Effectiveness Rating

3 = Text organizer was highly informative. It taught me a lot about the main idea.

2 = Text organizer was somewhat informative. I learned a little more about the main idea.

1 = Text organizer was not informative. I did not learn any more about the main idea.

Main idea of text #1	Main idea of text #2

Text #1   Text #2

Text organizers	Effectiveness rating	Text organizers	Effectiveness rating

Determine Importance—
Using Parts of the Book

Introduction

Nonfiction works focus on a particular topic and are intended to provide factual information through text and visual images. Unlike fictional works that may be based on fact but are crafted through a writer's imagination, a nonfiction text must contain accurate information that is verifiable from other sources. Nonfiction texts include a variety of organizational aids such as the preface, table of contents, glossary, appendix, and index. Strategic readers who learn to use these features will enhance their comprehension and understanding of informational texts.

- **Preface** (also known as the foreword or introduction): This section provides a lead-in for the author(s) to comment on why the book was written and provides clues as to the author's biases. This section will often contain details about the organization of the book and a suggestion about how best to read the book.

- **Table of Contents:** This part provides a "road map" of what the book contains by showing how the topics in the book are grouped. It provides an efficient system to find information included in a general topic. Look for texts that are organized in a logical, easy-to-follow manner.

- **Glossary:** This section provides definitions of difficult terms used in the text. It is essential in understanding the vocabulary of a difficult subject. It is a convenient aid for looking up technical and/or difficult terms.

- **Appendix:** An appendix provides additional information about a topic. It is located in the back of the book and contains information that supports and expands a chapter topic. The appendices may also be called "Student Almanac," "Reference," or "Reference Section."

- **Index:** This section provides the fastest means for locating topic-specific information referred to in the text. It directs the reader to specific pages of the text.

Using the Preface

The introductory material in the nonfiction book will be important in motivating students to continue reading. When you guide students through a preview of the book, make sure to spend time skimming and scanning the preface, introduction, and/or foreword. Inform students that a preface is a preliminary statement by the author or editor of the book, setting forth its purpose and scope, and sometimes expressing acknowledgment of assistance from others. Make sure students know that the acknowledgements section is sometimes separate and quite extensive. Have students think about the following questions as they preview the preface:

- What does the author want me to learn from this book?
- How does the information connect to what I already know?
- Does the content of the book sound interesting?
- What further research might I need to do in order to meet my purpose for reading?
- Am I clear about the general topics and concepts in the book?
- Do the tone and style of the writer connect with my own tone and style? Will I enjoy learning this information from this author?

Determine Importance—
Using Parts of the Book

Using the Table of Contents

Previewing the table of contents is one of the best tools for self-selecting a book. Make sure to take students to the school library and allow them to skim the tables of contents of several books when they have a new book project to complete or a new topic to research. Inform students that a table of contents is a list of the sections of the book with page numbers and that these sections may include: an introduction, acknowledgments, preface, foreword, chapter titles, appendix, glossary, and index. Some questions to guide the students through the previewing process include:

- What chapter title strikes me as the most interesting?
- Based on the title, what might I learn about the topic?
- How do these chapter titles connect to what I already know about the topic?
- How do the chapter titles build on each other?
- What will be my cumulative knowledge of the topic after reading this book?
- What chapter titles are missing? What information will I not gain from reading this book?
- Is this book worth my time? Will I achieve my purpose(s) for reading by delving into this book?

Using the Glossary

Glossaries are very helpful to students because they are essentially a dictionary specific to the nonfiction book that they are reading. The beauty of glossaries is that they are convenient and readily available since they are a part of the book. Often, motivated and proficient readers will make the extra effort to seek out a dictionary to define words and terms that they do not understand. However, struggling readers will most likely not make the effort to find a dictionary. Before exposing students to samples of glossaries, inform them that a glossary is a list of words with definitions intended to clarify the basic, technical, dialectical, and/or difficult terms found in the book. The glossary is usually located at the back of the book.

Using the Appendix

Appendices are very useful to readers who are trying to gain additional and substantive information on the topics and concepts presented in the book. Make sure to inform students that an appendix is a section of materials that supplements the main text of the book and is usually placed at the end. The appendix includes examples of various portions of the text and other information that is explanatory or bibliographic. The appendix material is useful, but the book is considered complete without it. Some useful questions to share with students include:

- How does the information in the appendix add to and extend the ideas in the book?
- What practical tips and ideas can I gain from the appendix?
- What statistical information, including charts, graphs, and diagrams, is included in the appendix?
- What is missing from the appendix? What would I like to know more about?
- What was the author thinking when he/she chose to include _____ in the appendix?
- Is any part of the appendix unnecessary? How so?
- How can I use the bibliographic information for further research?

Determine Importance—Using Parts of the Book

Using the Index

Teaching students that they have a catalog of information at their fingertips if they know how to use the index will greatly maximize their learning. Before practicing with indexes, inform students that an index is a detailed, alphabetical key to names, places, and topics in a book including references to their page location(s). Allow students many opportunities to learn that a specific term from the text may be explained several times, in several different ways, and in several different locations throughout the book. Model for students through think-alouds how to use the index, find the different locations for the term, read the different explanations, and determine which explanation best matches the purpose for reading. As a variation, divide students into partners and have them divide the responsibilities for finding the term in multiple locations in the text and determining the best explanation or definition. Students will appreciate the opportunity to discuss the merits of different explanations for a word that they don't understand or about which they need more information.

Using Strategies Independently

Throughout their academic careers, students will need to be able to select nonfiction books by previewing the various parts: introduction, preface, table of contents, appendix, index, glossary, etc. Be certain to guide students through this process by modeling for them how to use the parts of the book in order to make good decisions about which books will meet their purpose for reading. Provide opportunities for guided practice and make sure that students have opportunities to work in small groups or with a partner before they are expected to apply strategies independently. Build their confidence through praise and encouragement when they make wise book selections and display the ability to justify why they chose the book(s) that they did. During the first few weeks of school, spend a week focusing on one textbook at a time, using each of the strategies for a particular book. This process will lead students to a thorough understanding of each book before the need to use it arises.

Strategy 1: The Parts of a Textbook

Conduct a general overview of each organizational aid with students and explain how each aid can enhance learning. Distribute copies of page 193 for students to keep in their notebooks for future reference. (Standard 7.4)

Strategy 2: Using the Book Jacket

Examining the book jacket can yield useful information in deciding whether or not to keep reading. Inform students about the standard parts of the book jacket by referring them to the Using the Book Jacket activity on page 194. Model how to identify the various parts and discuss with them the effectiveness of the front cover, inside flaps, and back cover. Have them use the activity page to record key information for each part and then write a reaction in which they identify the information that matches their purpose for reading, connections to prior knowledge and personal experience, and any questions that they have. (Standards 5.2, 7.4, 7.6)

Determine Importance— Using Parts of the Book

Strategy 3: Using the Preface

Have students identify their purpose for reading, allow them to read the preface or introduction, and help them through discussion to understand the author's purpose for writing. Instruct them to use the activity page Using the Preface (page 195) to identify the background of the book, the major topics to be covered, the tone, and whether or not they would keep on reading. (Standards 5.2, 5.10, 7.4)

Strategy 4: Using the Foreword

Once students have identified their purpose for reading, have them use the activity page Using the Foreword (page 196) to identify key words and phrases, a prediction about what they will learn, how the information connects to their prior knowledge and purpose for reading, and any further questions that they have about the topic. Emphasize that the foreword, preface, and/or introduction all provide critical information to the reader that becomes the foundation for deciding whether or not to keep reading. (Standards 5.2, 5.10, 7.4, 7.6, 8.2)

Strategy 5: Converting the Table of Contents to Questions

Have students use the activity on page 197 to convert each of the chapter titles into a question. The example below shows how students may look at a table of contents and turn each title into a question to try to answer as they read:

Holiday Traditions Around the World

Table of Contents

Happy New Year! 1
Fun at Carnival 3
The Traditions of Passover 7
Independence Day for America 9
Dia De Los Muertos 11
Festivals of Light in Winter 13
Boxing Day 17

Convert Chapter Titles to Questions

Do all countries celebrate New Year's Day on the same day?

What is Carnival? What countries celebrate that day?

What are the traditions of Passover?

How do we know that the 4th of July is our Independence Day?

What language is Dia De Los Muertos? What does it mean?

What kinds of festivals happen in winter? Do they use a kind of light?

What is Boxing Day, and where is it celebrated?

Students read the chapter and record a general answer to the question. Then they identify at least one additional fact or detail that further elaborates on the general answer that they found. (Standard 7.4)

Determine Importance—
Using Parts of the Book

Strategy 6: Table of Contents

Have students complete the activity on page 198. (Standard 7.4)

Strategy 7: Glossary

Have students complete the activity on page 199, either independently or with a partner. (Standard 7.4)

Strategy 8: Glossary Practice

Have students complete page 200 for glossary practice. (Standard 7.4)

Strategy 9: Using the Glossary

Inform students that some nonfiction books have a built-in dictionary called a glossary. As they read, have them identify unfamiliar words by recording them on the Using the Glossary activity on page 201. Students then look up the words in the glossary and record the definitions on the activity page. Finally, have them reflect on how the definition helps to clarify their understanding of the text information. As a variation, have students create an illustrated mini-glossary (page 202). Have students read a short piece of nonfiction text, identify terms with which they are not familiar, use the glossary to create a short definition, and design a simple illustration or symbol to represent the newly learned word. Using art is motivating to students and will reinforce their understanding of the glossary. (Standard 7.4)

Strategy 10: Using the Appendix

Guide students in identifying their purpose for reading and allow them to select a nonfiction book to meet that purpose. Provide students with the activity on page 203 and have them select five to eight topics from the appendix that match their purpose for reading (or simply look interesting). Have them record the topics, page numbers, and definitions or key words in the chart. Allow students an opportunity to work with a partner on this activity. Then, have students preview the rest of the book and determine information that might be missing from the appendix. Instruct them to discuss and describe an addition to the appendix that they could create with a partner. After reading the book, you might want to have them design this addition to the appendix as a culminating or supplementary activity to show their comprehensive knowledge of the subject. You can be certain that students will gain much information if they are able to determine what information is missing. As a follow-up to this activity, students can use the activity on page 204 to locate additional information using the appendix. (Standards 5.1, 5.2, 7.4)

Strategy 11: Using the Index

Help students to understand their purpose for reading. Have them use the activity on page 205 to record unfamiliar words/terms. Instruct students to use the index to find additional sources of information from the book and record the page numbers on the activity page. After students have investigated each of the page numbers, they can reflect on the information they found most useful. This information can be in the form of facts, details, examples, illustrations, charts, etc. Allow for the possibility that none of the additional places in the text were useful. Encourage students to discuss the remaining questions or confusion they have and strategies for finding the information they need. (Standards 5.2, 7.4)

Determine Importance—
Using Parts of the Book

Strategy 12: Create a Poster

Have the group of students who are studying the preface create a poster of important facts about the preface. They can title it "What You Should Know about the Preface." Have students creatively list important facts that they should know about the preface. They can include where it is found, if it is listed in the table of contents, what is explained in it, who writes it, and why it is important to comprehension of the text. See page 206. (Standard 7.4)

Strategy 13: Group Posters

This cooperative learning strategy is a great way for getting students to take ownership of their learning. Divide the class into five different groups, and assign a different part of the book to each group. The group members will discuss how they can best convey, in poster form, the information contained in their assigned part of the book. Provide the groups with a poster board and markers, and give them an adequate amount of time to complete their posters. Once posters are complete, the groups are to write a specified number of questions to check for understanding of their poster. A group member should then neatly write the questions on a blank overhead transparency. Groups present their poster, answer questions to provide clarification, and then put their "check for understanding" questions on the overhead projector to present an oral exam. (Standards 7.4, 8.2)

Strategy 14: Morning Warm-Ups

Focus on information in a particular textbook as a part of Morning Warm-Ups. Each day write a question on the board for students to answer. (Standards 7.3, 7.4) Examples:

- What part of your social studies textbook would you use to look up information about the Louisiana Purchase?
- Which chapter in your health textbook is about fire safety?
- What kind of information is contained in Appendix II of your math textbook?
- Look on page 547 of your science textbook. What is that section called, and how is it useful?

Strategy 15: All Students Respond

This strategy can be used for just a few minutes each day to practice and reinforce the use of the parts of a textbook for locating information. For each student, punch a hole in the upper left-hand corner of five index cards, and place the cards on a ring. Have students write one of the following terms on each card: table of contents, glossary, index, preface, and appendix. On a regular basis, ask students to hold up the correct cards to indicate the correct answers to your questions regarding parts of the book. A session would go something like this: "Take out your parts-of-the-book response cards, and listen carefully to my questions. What part of the book would you use to find out what a 'plateau' is?" (Students should respond with their "glossary" cards.) "Good, I see that most of you have responded with the 'glossary' card. Will someone please tell us why you would look in the glossary?" Continue in this fashion by asking a question, waiting an adequate amount of time for all students to respond, checking for accuracy, and then asking students to articulate why a particular answer is correct. (Standard 7.4)

Determine Importance— Using Parts of the Book

The Parts of a Textbook

Learning about the parts of your textbook and the information found in those parts will help you become a better reader. When you get a new textbook, carefully inspect each of these parts.

Preface

- This part of the book is located in the very beginning of the book.
- It is sometimes called the foreword or the introduction.
- In this section, the author of the book comments on why the book was written.
- Reading this section will tell you how the book is organized.
- The preface may also have a suggestion about how best to read the book.

Table of Contents

- The table of contents shows you the page numbers for units, chapters, glossary, index, and appendix.
- It is the first place you look when you want to find out where a specific section begins.

Glossary

- The glossary is like a dictionary that is found at the back of many textbooks.
- It contains some of the important words used in the textbook along with their definitions.
- Like a dictionary, the words in the glossary are listed in alphabetical order.

Index

- With an index, you can find specific pages that tell about people, places, and things that are in the textbook.
- It also lists the page numbers for diagrams, graphs, maps, illustrations, photos, and tables.
- The index is found at the back of the book, and the information is listed in alphabetical order.

Appendix

- Sometimes a textbook will contain an appendix. More than one appendix are called appendices.
- The appendices contain special information about the topics in the textbook. A math textbook might contain appendices that have tables of different measurements or conversion tables. A social studies textbook appendix might have lists of presidents or state populations.

Determine Importance—Using Parts of the Book

Using the Book Jacket

Directions: Identify your purpose for reading and then preview the book jacket for key information. In the chart below, record the parts of the book jacket in the left column and the information that you found that matches your purpose for reading in the right column.

Parts of a book jacket:

Front cover: illustration, title, author
Inside flaps: preview of the content of the book and information about the author
Back cover: recommendations and possibly more information about the content of the book

Purpose for reading: _____

_____

Part of the book cover and key information	Reaction: How does this information match your purpose for reading? What is your prior knowledge or personal experience that connects to the information? What questions do you have?

Determine Importance—Using Parts of the Book

Using the Preface

Directions: Use the following activity page to analyze the preface of a nonfiction book.

Definition of a preface: a preliminary statement by the author or editor of a book, setting forth its purpose and scope, expressing acknowledgment of assistance from others, etc.

Purpose for reading: _____

_____

Author's purpose: _____

Description of the background of the book (may include where the idea of the book came from): _____

_____

_____

_____

What are the major topics covered in the book (scope)? _____

_____

_____

What is the tone of the book (formal/informal, informative/entertaining, chatty/serious, etc.)? Explain. _____

_____

_____

_____

Will you keep reading based on the preface? Explain. _____

_____

_____

_____

Determine Importance— Using Parts of the Book

Using the Foreword

Directions: Use the following activity page to analyze the foreword of a nonfiction text.

Definition of a foreword: an introduction or preface to the book

Purpose for reading: _____

_____

What are the key words or phrases from the foreword?	What do you predict that you will learn?
How will this information connect to your prior knowledge and/or your purpose for reading?	What questions do you have about the topic based on the foreword?

Determine Importance— Using Parts of the Book

Converting the Table of Contents to Questions

Directions: Change the chapter titles to questions. Record a general answer and at least one additional fact or detail.

Definition of a table of contents: a list of the sections of the book with page numbers (sections include: introduction, acknowledgments, preface, foreword, chapter titles, appendix, glossary, index, etc.)

Convert chapter title to a question	General answer	One additional fact or detail

Determine Importance— Using Parts of the Book

Table of Contents

Directions: Read the table of contents below. Use the information to answer the questions.

1. In which chapter will you find a story about turtles? _____

2. In which chapter will you find funny stories?_____

3. Which chapter will leave you guessing until the end? _____

4. If you are reading on page 16, what story are you reading? _____

5. If you are reading on page 26, what story are you reading? _____

6. On what page will you find the beginning of the story "Who Did It?" _____

7. On what page will you find the beginning of the story "The Horse in the River?" _____

8. What story (stories) would you predict to take place in the water? _____

9. What story (stories) would you predict will involve jewelry?_____

10. According to this table of contents, how many stories are in this book? _____

Determine Importance— Using Parts of the Book

Glossary

Directions: Read the glossary below and fill in the missing words.

Glossary

atmosphere (n.) The layer of air and other gases that surround the earth

efficient (adj.) Working without wasting a lot of energy

gravity (n.) The force that pulls objects to the center of the earth and planets to the sun

momentum (n.) The force that keeps a moving object moving in the same direction

temperature (n.) A level of heat

transport (v.) To move from one place to another

vehicle (n.) A machine used for transporting people or materials

---

1. The rocket was used to _____ the materials to the space station.

2. The lack of _____ causes astronauts to float in the spacecraft.

3. What is the _____ of the sun in degrees Fahrenheit?

Directions: Answer the following questions based on the glossary above.

4. How many nouns are listed in this glossary?_____

5. Write the adjective(s): _____

6. Between which two words would the definition for "rocket" go?

   _____

7. Between which two words would the definition for "thermometer" go?

   _____

8. What might be a good title for the book? _____

Determine Importance—
Using Parts of the Book

Glossary Practice

Directions: Find the glossary in your book. Choose five words that you didn't know before. List them in alphabetical order. Find a sentence from the book with each word you chose. Copy the sentence on the line provided. Now write your own sentence using each word.

Glossary words

1. _____

2. _____

3. _____

4. _____

5. _____

Sentences copied from the book

1. _____

2. _____

3. _____

4. _____

5. _____

Your own sentences

1. _____

2. _____

3. _____

4. _____

5. _____

Determine Importance—
Using Parts of the Book

Using the Glossary

Directions: As you read, record words with which you are unfamiliar. Look up these words in the glossary and record the definitions in your own words. Then explain how the definitions help you to clarify the text information.

Definition of a glossary: a list of words with definitions intended to clarify the basic, technical, and/or difficult terms found in the book

Terms/words with which you are unfamiliar	Definition in your own words	How does this definition help to clarify your understanding of the text information?

Determine Importance—Using Parts of the Book

Creating an Illustrated Mini-Glossary

Directions: Use the following activity to create an illustrated mini-glossary that will help the reader to better understand the text information. As you read, highlight or underline words that you do not understand. Then, record the words below, look them up in a dictionary, and restate the definition in a simpler way in your own words. Finally, create an illustration or symbol to represent the word.

Term or word	Brief definition	Illustration or symbol

Determine Importance—
Using Parts of the Book

Using the Appendix

Directions: Identify your purpose for reading, select a nonfiction book, and preview the appendix. Select five to eight topics that match your purpose for reading. Record the topics and the page numbers in the chart. Then look up each topic and record the definition or key words and phrases about the topic.

Definition of an appendix: a section of materials that supplements the main text of the book and is usually placed at the end. The appendix includes examples of various portions of the text, as well as other information that is explanatory or bibliographic. The appendix material is useful, but the book is considered complete without it.

Purpose for reading: _____

_____

Topic	Page number	Definition or key words and phrases from the text to describe the topic

Determine Importance—
Using Parts of the Book

Locating Additional Information Using the Appendix

Directions: As you read, record interesting or important information from the text. Underline key words and phrases. Then, identify any questions you have in the center column. Using a supplemental text, find the answers to your questions in the appendix. Remember to use the key words you highlighted from the left column to help you locate additional information.

Title of Text: _____

Supplemental Text: _____

Interesting or important information from the original text	Questions I have	Supplemental text information—record key words from the appendix and page number location

Determine Importance—
Using Parts of the Book

Using the Index

Directions: Begin by identifying your purpose for reading. As you read, record unfamiliar words or terms. Use the index to locate additional sources of information. Record the facts, details, and examples in the book that best helped you to understand the unfamiliar word or term and helped you achieve your purpose for reading.

Definition of an index: a detailed alphabetical key to names, places, and topics in a book, including references to their page location(s)

Purpose for reading: _____

_____

Unfamiliar word or term	Page numbers where additional information can be found	Information that is most useful (details, facts, examples)

Determine Importance—Using Parts of the Book

Create a Poster

Preface

Directions: Create a poster that shows all of the important information about the preface. Include a title, such as "What You Should Know about the Preface." Be sure to include all information your group has found. Ideas include, but are not limited to:

- Where is it found?
- How can you find it?
- What information is in it?
- Who wrote it?
- Why is it important?
- Personal responses to prefaces you have read

List all of your ideas on a sheet of scratch paper first. Check all spelling and punctuation. Brainstorm the layout and any art you might want to include. Now it is time to make your poster. Use your best printing. When you are done, ask your teacher to display the poster for the rest of the class to see.

Appendix

Directions: Create a poster that shows all of the important information about the appendix. Include a title, such as "What You Should Know about the Appendix." Be sure to include all information your group has found. Ideas include, but are not limited to:

- Where is it found?
- How can you find it?
- What information is in it?
- Why is it important?
- Personal responses to appendices you have read

List all of your ideas on a sheet of scratch paper first. Check all spelling and punctuation. Brainstorm the layout and any art you might want to include. Now it is time to make your poster. Use your best printing. When you are done, ask your teacher to display the poster for the rest of the class to see.

Visualize

PASSPORT TO COMPREHENSION

Visualize

Introduction

When students strengthen their ability to visualize, they create the building blocks for proficiency in making inferences. Teachers need to be aware that students can use words from text, titles, charts, diagrams, and illustrations to make inferences and thus improve their ability to understand the information. An effective approach for presenting the idea of making inferences is to share with students some specific descriptions or scenarios and have them make an inference about the events in the scenario. For example, a young girl comes home from school crying and places a paper with a red mark on the kitchen table for her mother to see. Students will infer that the girl received a poor grade on a test or project. After presenting students with many such scenarios, their confidence with this skill will improve.

Next, you can move on to making inferences with text. Share with students some descriptive scenarios from text that create a visual picture in their minds. For example, the author describes a scene where a group of baseball players leave the baseball field, give each other high fives, and lift the pitcher into the air and onto their shoulders. The reader can infer that the team won the game and that the pitcher was an integral part of this victory. To build the connection between visualizing and making inferences, have the students create a picture in their minds of the scene that happened before the victory and describe it in detail. Filling in the missing information will help students comprehend textual information, and it is a technique that they can transfer across subject areas.

Using Prior Knowledge

An excellent way to tap into prior knowledge and make the connection to visualization is through guided practice with previewing text. Before you have students begin reading, have them look carefully at the title and identify any visual images associated with the words in the title. Then, students can preview the text, noting the headings, subheadings, charts, graphs, and illustrations. Again, have them identify visual images associated with these various text features. It may be helpful to record all of these observations on the board. Finally, have students make connections between the visual images they have identified and their prior knowledge of the topic. As students read the text, make sure to refer them to their initial visualizations and connections to prior knowledge. Ask them to revise or clarify their understandings as they gain new information about the topic.

Visualize

Sensory Detail

Proficient readers use sensory details to make pictures in their minds. These readers are able to use details to see, hear, taste, touch, and smell the images that are described in the text. It is essential for teachers to model how to create pictures in one's mind when reading. Proficient readers create mental images but often don't realize what is going on cognitively in order for them to "see" the text. Teachers must help proficient readers understand the visualizing skills that they have developed in order to further build on these skills. Additionally, they must help struggling readers to use sensory details to begin the process of visualizing text.

Creating Mental Images to Remember Details

Retention is a critical component of reading comprehension. As proficient readers enter the text world and begin to form vague pictures of the big ideas, they will also begin to add distinctive impressions of the details. As educators, we often ask students to simply retain the facts, the details, and the small ideas. It is important to teach students that building a strong ability to visualize will help them to retain the big idea(s) and provide the scaffolding on which to hang the details. When we assess students' progress, it is extremely valuable to incorporate many kinds of evaluation. A unit test may include some multiple choice, true/false, short-answer, and long-answer responses. In addition to the traditional approaches to assessment, make sure to include a question that asks students to reflect upon how they used visualization to remember key concepts, facts, and details. Such a component of assessment will help students build their metacognitive abilities and ultimately strengthen their retention of information.

Creating Mental Images to Draw Conclusions

Drawing conclusions is a skill essential to all subject areas. Have students use proven strategies to visualize text information and draw conclusions about what the author is trying to teach them about the topic. Be sure to have students identify the specific text information and inferential information that allowed them to draw the conclusion that they did.

Incorporating New Information

One of the key features of learning and teaching is that new information builds on what is already known. If students gain proficiency with linking new information to what they already know about the topic and making connections across contexts and subject areas, then their learning will improve exponentially. The following are some questions that you can ask students to help them both build their visualizing skills and make connections in order to incorporate new information into their existing knowledge base.

Visualize

Incorporating New Information *(cont.)*

Before Reading

- What do you already know about the topic?
- What images do you already have that connect with your current knowledge or understanding of the topic?
- Can you describe these images?
- Can you represent these images either through art or drama?

During Reading

- What new information are you learning about the topic?
- What images do you associate with this new information?
- Can you describe these images?
- How do these new images confirm or contradict the images that you identified before you began reading?

After Reading

- What key information (concepts, topics, facts) did you learn?
- Have you blended your existing images about the topic with the new images?
- Can you represent the connections you have made between your existing knowledge and new knowledge through art or drama?
- How does visualizing improve the learning process?

Using Strategies Independently

What follows is a list of strategies designed to improve students' visualization abilities when reading. Make sure to model for students how to visualize through think-alouds in which you share with students the images you create in your mind as you read and the thinking that accompanies your sense-making. Demonstrate for students how to use each strategy on the board and/or overhead. Most importantly, share with students your enthusiasm for reading and the confusion and misconceptions that you encounter when reading. Gradually release the responsibility for using strategies to students by observing carefully their proficiency and confidence levels with each new strategy you present.

Visualize

Strategy 1: Can You Name That Thing?

This activity will highlight the frustration of trying to read a passage without visualizing. Without giving any hints, read aloud this passage:

> First you carry the thing to where you need it. Then you pull its legs apart and push down its latches. You go up it and do something. When you are done, you come down backwards. Then you release the latches, push its legs together, and put it away.

Ask for ideas about the passage. As students offer ideas, ask them what words or phrases from the passage triggered their ideas. Some students will be completely baffled by this description; since they had no idea what part of their memories to access, they didn't form any visual images and, as a result, could make no sense of the passage. Now tell them the clue word, "climb," and reread the passage. Most of the students will immediately recognize the use of a stepladder. Explain that once they were able to access their memories of things that people climb, they were able to get a visual of what was happening. Follow up by having the students draw the stepladder. (Standard 5.5)

Strategy 2: Imagine What's Missing

Using clues from the illustrations, skillful readers imagine the missing pictures that link the illustrations together to make the story make sense. Go through a wordless picture book with the class, looking at and discussing the pictures. Ask students to draw what they visualize happening between two of the pictures and write a sentence to go with it. For example, in the book *Tuesday* by David Wiesner, there is a picture of a frog on a flying lily pad being chased by a big dog. In the next illustration the dog is fleeing from a squadron of frogs on flying lily pads. Your quick scan of each student's drawing of the missing event (the dog turning around when he sees all the frogs coming) will enable you to immediately detect misconceptions so that you can address problems quickly. You can find other good examples in any of the series of Carl books by Alexandra Day. After this activity, have students complete "Imagine What's Missing" on page 217. This page has panels with illustrations missing. The students need to provide the missing event(s). (Standard 5.1)

Strategy 3: Visual Vocabulary

Prepare a list of vocabulary from an upcoming expository passage. Present the seven to ten most important words that can be visualized or can evoke sensory images. Avoid concept words like liberty and equality for which students cannot generate visual or sensory images. For example, if you are reading about caverns, you might select these words: *cold*, *dark*, *damp*, *dripping water*, *spelunker*, *stalagmite*, *stalactite*, *cave*, *labyrinth*. Have students stare for 30 seconds at a picture of one word. Then they close their eyes and recreate that picture in their minds. Do the same for each vocabulary word that can be illustrated. For words that cannot be illustrated (e.g., damp), you can pass around a damp cloth, turn on a faucet so that it drips water, etc. (Standard 5.1)

Visualize

Strategy 4: Mini-Skit Planner

Mini-skits allow students to summarize what they have learned through drama. Have the students use the planning sheet (page 218) to identify characters, concepts, and facts that they will incorporate into their mini-drama. Then, instruct them to plan a brief dialogue that demonstrates the relationship(s) between ideas. Mini-skits are a great technique to help students build their visualization skills. (Standard 7.5)

Strategy 5: Newscast Planner

Planning a newscast will get students involved in writing reports, editorializing, and interviewing characters in order to demonstrate their knowledge of a particular concept or idea. Have students use the activity page (page 219) to plan their newscast in cooperative groups. (Standards 7.5, 7.6)

Strategy 6: Symbolic Story Representations

Symbolic story representations (Enciso 1992) involve a technique in which students are given different pieces of colored construction paper and use the paper to tear shapes that represent different ideas, concepts, or characters from the text. Then, students arrange the shapes on a large piece of construction paper in order to show the relationships between or among the ideas. Finally, students explain their creations in small groups or through written responses. The simple act of tearing shapes is highly motivating to students and is a nonthreatening way for them to represent their ideas, since little to no artistic ability is required. (Standards 7.5, 7.6)

Strategy 7: Storyboard Planner

An essential step in the planning process of movies and TV shows, storyboarding is a great way for students to visualize the sequence of steps in a scientific experiment or the events that unfolded during a particular time in history. Introduce the idea of storyboarding to students by showing them the activity on page 220 and having them think about a sequence of events or steps with which they are familiar. For example, their morning routine before coming to school can be set up as a storyboard. Then, have students read the text and illustrate through symbols and simple illustrations the sequence or steps in the text. (Standard 7.7)

Strategy 8: Making a Postcard

Having students visualize various audiences helps them to strengthen their reading skills. Instruct students to use the activity on page 221 to create a postcard that demonstrates a relationship between characters or ideas in the text. Students will have to use their skill of making inferences to conceive of such an interaction and their skill of visualization to imagine the sender, receiver, and location that the postcard depicts. In social studies, examples include the creation of postcards exchanged between historical figures. In science, examples include postcards that show the interaction between neutrons and protons, veins and arteries, or animals that occupy the same habitat. (Standard 7.6)

Visualize

Strategy 9: Listening to Music

When introducing the skills of visualizing, using music is an effective strategy. Classical music, such as Vivaldi's *The Four Seasons* or Beethoven's *Fifth Symphony*, will evoke many images in students' minds. Begin by giving students the guide for listening to music (page 222) and instructing them to record as many images as possible as they listen to the music. You may need to demonstrate this procedure with a short piece of music before students begin. For example, a fast-paced selection of music with a lively rhythm might evoke the image of fairies dancing in the woods and playing hide-and-seek. After the students finish listening to the music and recording their images, have them use the right side of the listening guide to write a brief story, poem, or description that incorporates the images. Make sure to point out to students that they need to transfer the ability to visualize while listening to music to their reading. (Standard 7.6)

Strategy 10: Text Graphing

Text graphing allows students to visualize the information they are learning as well as evaluate it. This technique is particularly effective to use with social studies. Have students list the events that they are encountering in the text. Next, have them think of an artistic representation or symbol for each of the events. Then present them with the Text Graphing activity on page 223, and have them evaluate each of the events by drawing their symbols to correspond with the appropriate number on the graph. For example, the American's defeat of the British at the Battle of Yorktown might be evaluated as a +4 because of the American's victory, but not receive a +5 rating because many lives were lost in the process. It is important to note that there aren't any "right" or "wrong" answers in text graphing and that different students may rate events differently. Students should be encouraged to justify their ratings either in writing, or in small-group or whole-group discussions. (Standard 7.6)

Strategy 11: Visualizing Parts of Speech

This is a simple technique that reinforces parts of speech and requires students to categorize the images that they are encountering. Present students with the parts-of-speech organizer (page 224) and have them record specific nouns, vivid verbs, interesting adjectives, and exciting adverbs as they read. To enrich this activity, have the students write an original description using the words that they found in the text. (Standard 5.7)

Strategy 12: Questions for Visualizing Text

Provide the list of questions on page 225 for students to use while reading. Students can keep this list of questions in their reading journals to remind them to visualize when reading. Discuss each of the questions prior to handing out the list to make sure students understand them. (Standard 5.8)

Strategy 13: Visualize While Reading

Create a transparency of page 226, and model the thinking processes for students as the corresponding sensory responses are filled in. For example, as you read a passage from a textbook describing an event in history, stop frequently to think aloud and describe what you are visualizing. Include a great deal of detail in your descriptions and emphasize how pausing to reflect on these images helps you understand the text better. Note how your images change as you read further and how these images help to create your own meaning for the text. Continue reading and adding details as you go. As you fill in the overhead transparency, students can copy the responses onto their own copies. Keep multiple copies of page 226 available, and encourage students to use them whenever they read something new. (Standard 5.8)

Strategy 14: Making Analogies

For this strategy, students make comparisons between something that is known and familiar and something that is unknown. As a morning starter, write an analogy on the board related to a topic that you are currently studying. Have students copy the analogy into their journals or learning logs and then solve it. Additionally, require students to write about the analogy, how they solved it, and what they thought about or visualized as they solved it. The activity on page 227 can be duplicated and used for additional student practice. (Standard 5.7)

Strategy 15: Real-Life Comparisons

Nonfiction text in the content areas often depends on the notions of size, weight, length, distance, and time to covey relevant facts. Visualizing when reading nonfiction texts can involve making comparisons between new concepts and something familiar to students. For example, if a student reads that a Pilgrim family of five lived in a one-room home that measured 10 feet by 12 feet, students may not have a reliable concept of this situation. To facilitate visualization of these cramped quarters, map out the area on the floor with masking tape or on concrete with chalk. Ask five students to stand together in the "model" and act out tasks such as cooking, washing, eating, sleeping, etc. This activity will give students an idea of how cramped the living quarters were at that time in history. Imagine how much more extensively a student could answer an inferential question, such as "What would it be like for you to live in the time of the Pilgrims? Explain how your life would be." (Standard 7.6)

Strategy 16: Inside the Picture

Science and social studies texts are loaded with illustrations and graphics to help students to understand new and unfamiliar concepts. To ensure that students can begin visualizing the moment they begin reading such text, always preview a chapter with a "text walk," paying special attention to pictures and photographs. Add a visualization element to the text walk by stopping at a photo and having students concentrate on it. Say, "Don't look away from the photo. You have now entered the photo. What do you see? smell? hear? taste? What do you feel (emotion)? Now you are coming out of the photo. Let's discuss our experiences." (Standard 5.1)

Visualize

Strategy 17: SCAMPER

This activity is a good strategy for getting students to expand their thinking and visualization skills. It will encourage them to expand ideas or develop them into completely new possibilities; it will foster creativity when they have trouble coming up with ideas or when all the ideas seem to be very similar; and it will help students expand their observational skills and sharpen their five senses.

SCAMPER stands for:

- **S**ubstitute: What could be used instead?

- **C**ombine: What could be added?

- **A**dapt: How can it be adjusted to suit a condition or purpose?

- **M**odify: How can the color, shape, or form be changed?

- or Magnify: How can it be made larger, stronger, or thicker?

- or Minify: How can it be made smaller, lighter, or shorter?

- **P**ut to other use: What else can it be used for other than the original intended purpose?

- **E**liminate: What can be removed or taken away from it?

- **R**everse: How can it be turned around or placed opposite its original position?

- or Rearrange: How can the pattern, order, or layout be changed?

When introducing this strategy to students, begin by using only one or two of the letters at a time. It is not necessary to use the letters/words in the order they are listed. "P," (put to other uses) and "M," (modify, magnify, or minify) are often good starting points. Use the graphic organizer on page 228 for this activity. (Standard 5.1)

Strategy 18: Draw the Story

Invite a storyteller to come to your class and tell a story. (African and American Indian folktales are especially good.) Ask students to draw the most important or interesting mental image created as they were listening. (Standard 8.16)

Strategy 19: Comparing Pictures

Set up a listening center filled with illustrated books on tape. Have students listen to the tape two times before they even see the book's cover. Then they read the book, either with the tape's support or independently. Ask them to fill in a Venn diagram. Label one side "Book's Pictures" and the other side "My Mind's Pictures." (Standard 7.6)

Visualize

Imagine What's Missing

Directions: Draw pictures to complete each story.

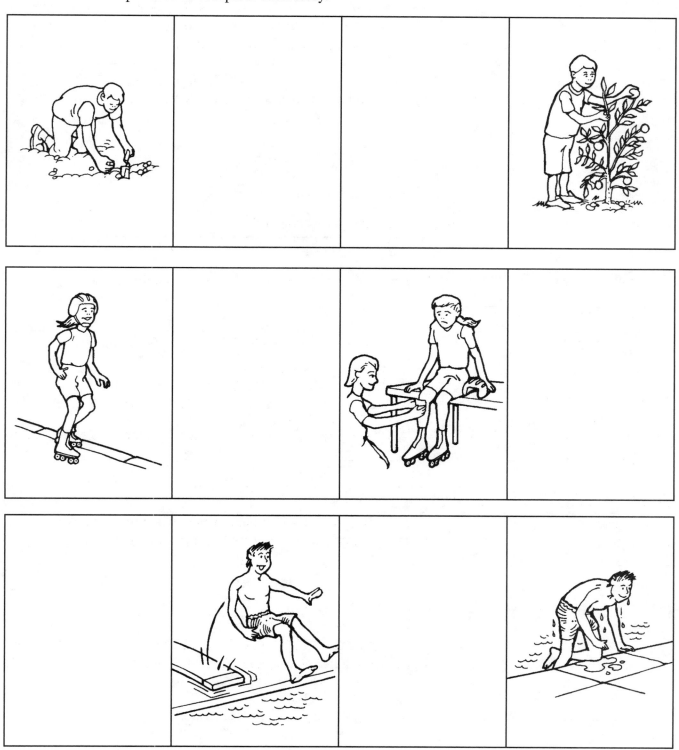

Visualize

Mini-Skit Planner

Directions: With your team member(s), plan out a mini-skit that dramatizes what you have read.

Student Names	Characters	Main Character Traits

Key concept(s) you will dramatize: _____

_____

_____

Facts from your learning: _____

_____

_____

Dialogue that shows key concepts, facts learned, and relationships among ideas:

_____

_____

_____

_____

_____

_____

_____

_____

_____

_____

Visualize

Newscast Planner

Directions: Use the following graphic organizer to plan a newscast with your team that shows the knowledge that you have gained about the topic or concept you are studying.

Student Names	Newscast Names	Newscast Topic

Visual aids that will be used in the newscast to illustrate the topics learned:

_____

_____

_____

Each of the newscast members will have to plan a newscast story that shows the following information about the topic learned. Each member will want to use separate lined notebook paper to plan and write the newscast story. Use the following questions to guide you.

➤ Who are the main characters in the newscast story? (historical figures in social studies; chemicals or elements in science; signs or symbols in mathematics)

➤ What is their interaction? What is the problem?

➤ When did this interaction or problem occur?

➤ Where?

➤ Why?

➤ How?

Visualize

Storyboard Planner

Directions: Use the following planner to illustrate the events, process, or steps as they occurred in the text. Be creative!

Event #1	Event #2	Event #3
Event #4	Event #5	Event #6
Event #7	Event #8	Event #9
Event #10	Event #11	Event #12

Visualize

Making a Postcard

Directions: Use the graphic organizer below to plan a postcard that is sent from one person or idea in the text to another person or idea. Use the first box to illustrate the location from which the postcard is sent. Use the second box to plan the message from sender to receiver.

Front of Postcard

Back of Postcard

(Message)

(Stamp)

(Address)

Visualize

Listening to Music

Directions: As you listen to the music, record as many images as you can in the left column of the chart. When the music is finished, write a response using the images. This response can be in the form of a creative short story, a poem, or a description of a memory.

Images from the music	Response (short story, poem, description of a memory, etc.) Be as creative and descriptive as possible.

Visualize

Text Graphing

Directions: Use the following chart to illustrate the events in the text. Events that are positive are to be illustrated in the top half of the chart and events that are negative are to be illustrated in the bottom half of the chart. Use the +5 to –5 rating system to indicate the degree of positive or negative associated with the event. The center horizontal line is "0."

Positive Events

+5

+4

+3

+2

+1

Negative Events

-1

-2

-3

-4

-5

Visualize

Visualizing Parts of Speech

Directions: As you are reading, record specific nouns, vivid verbs, interesting adjectives, and exciting adverbs in the appropriate parts of the chart.

Specific nouns	Vivid verbs
Interesting adjectives	**Exciting adverbs**

Do you think the author did a good job creating a picture in your head using different parts of speech? Explain.

_____

_____

_____

_____

_____

Visualize

Questions for Visualizing Text

Directions: Use the following questions to help you visualize the text.

1. What pictures are you forming in your mind of people, places, things, and ideas?

2. What details from the text are helping you to create a picture in your mind?

3. What details from your own experience are you adding to the picture in your own mind?

4. If you were to make a movie using the pictures in your mind, what would you use for background music?

5. If you were to make a movie using the pictures in your mind, what colors and shading would you use to represent mood?

6. Are you seeing in your mind what the author intended you to see? Why do you think so?

7. How would you describe the pictures or images in your mind to a friend?

8. Do you see yourself interacting with the people, places, things, or ideas that you are visualizing in your mind? Explain.

9. What images or details are missing from the text? Can you fill in these images in your own mind?

10. Do the images that you see in your mind based on text information remind you of a personal memory? Explain.

11. Do the images and ideas in your mind remind you of other texts that you have read on the same topic? Explain.

12. What if a major idea in the text were deleted? How would this change the pictures in your mind?

13. If you were to paint a picture of a major idea from the text, what would it look like? What colors and textures would you use?

14. Imagine a dialogue between people or ideas in the text. What is the content of the dialogue? What is the voice/tone of the people or ideas?

15. How does visualizing ideas from the text help you to make inferences?

Visualize

Visualize While Reading

Directions: Fill in your responses to your reading.

Topic:_____ Page number(s): _____

I see...	I smell...
I can taste...	I hear...

I can feel...

Visualize

Making Analogies

Directions: Writing your own analogies can help you to understand the relationships between words and ideas. Look at the first two words that are given and picture the relationship between the two of them. Use a dictionary if you are not sure what a word means. Next, think of two other words that have the same relationship. The first one is done for you.

1. trout : fish :: _____*parrot*_____ : _____*bird*_____

2. geyser : steam :: _____ : _____

3. bee : buzz :: _____ : _____

4. butterfly : monarch :: _____ : _____

5. flock : sheep :: _____ : _____

6. sphygmomanometer : blood pressure :: _____ : _____

7. quart : pint :: _____ : _____

8. wind velocity : anemometer :: _____ : _____

9. wolf : cub :: _____ : _____

10. geologist : minerals :: _____ : _____

Visualize

SCAMPER

Directions: Use this chart to sharpen your observational skills. Fill in the chart after your teacher discusses each column.

S Substitute	**C** Combine	**A** Adapt	**M** Modify Magnify Minify	**P** Put to other uses	**E** Eliminate	**R** Reverse Rearrange

Summarize and Synthesize

Summarize and Synthesize

Introduction

Reading a text, deciding on the important ideas in the text, and putting them together in one's own words is summarizing. Summarizing requires students to be able to pick out only the most important ideas and tell about them. Students often have a difficult time separating what is important from what is not so important. They tend to retell all parts of a text, often focusing on the most interesting ideas rather than the most important ones. Teaching students how to read for understanding and to summarize text is a higher-level thinking skill. It also sets a purpose for reading, actively involving students during reading. Paraphrasing is the process of restating what was read in one's own words. Paraphrasing is a way for students to tell the main ideas of a text in their own words, which may make the text easier for them to understand. Synthesizing requires students to take new information, compare it to what they already know, and make speculations or draw conclusions.

Reading for Important Facts

Nonfiction texts can be highly motivating to students because the content is often interesting, and the presentation of the material is attractive and stimulating. However, it is important that students be able to distill the essence of the information and retain key concepts and facts in order to maximize their learning. Previewing the information for text features and skimming and scanning the content can help readers to focus on the facts. Here are some ideas to help students:

- Tap into students' prior knowledge on the subject. Ask questions about facts they already know.

- Have students preview the text for length and format.

- Lead students through a brief discussion of headings and subheadings. Have them link this information to the facts that they already know.

- If the text has many features such as graphs, charts, and photographs, help them to create an "attack" plan. Help them decide what order in which to read all of the information.

- Model for students how to decide if the text should be carefully read or simply skimmed for facts and key information.

- Help students decide what is less relevant information.

Selecting Significant Text Information

After students preview the text and delve into the reading, it is essential that they know how to recognize important information. Remind students to pay particular attention to the following text features:

- headings and subheadings
- bold words
- italicized words
- captions
- illustrations

- photographs
- charts
- graphs
- maps
- labels

Summarize and Synthesize

Selecting Significant Text Information *(cont.)*

Model for students how to ask questions as they read in order to identify significant text information:

- What are the key concepts?
- What are the main ideas?
- What are the important facts?
- How does the information I am reading connect to what I am learning in class?
- How do the text features help me to understand what's significant?

Provide students with several note-taking forms so that as they read they can select significant text information. In addition, model for them how to use codes (page 250) to mark important information in the text as they read.

Organizing Information

There are many ways for students to organize the information that they encounter. Some of the more traditional approaches include outlining and using note cards. It is important to teach students how to use traditional approaches, but it is also important to show them various techniques to allow for diverse learning styles in the classroom. Some of these techniques include webbing, double-entry journals, and concept mapping. Given the amount of information that students will interact with over the course of their education, it is essential that they are able to have various tools to sort information into key concepts, main ideas, and supporting details. Unfortunately, not all texts can be so neatly sorted into these three categories; therefore, the approaches that you share with students should allow for flexibility and adaptation.

Using Strategies Independently

As students progress through their education, they will need to have proficiency in a variety of skills to help them recognize, organize, and respond to vast amounts of factual information. Remember to model for students how to use the strategies to help them make sense of the big and small ideas that they will encounter. With careful monitoring and support, allow students to take responsibility for finding and making sense of text information.

Strategy 1: Illustration Summaries

To get students started with the skill of summarizing, tell them the definition of summarizing: retelling, in a shorter version than the original, only the most important information. Read to students a short piece of nonfiction text and tell them to think about the most important information. Then give students a blank sheet of paper and have them draw a picture of the key ideas in the text. They can be as creative as they want and use captions or labels, but they are not to write a paragraph. When students are finished, have them share their artistic creations with the class. Keep track of the students' ideas on the overhead or on the board, and look for commonalities among their understandings of what is most important. (Standard 7.5)

Summarize and Synthesize

Strategy 2: Note-Taking Wheel

Note-taking wheels are particularly useful with nonfiction text that is organized in a narrative fashion as texts often are in social studies. Using the template on page 237, students can record important people, events, settings, and other facts. When students finish, have them share their wheels with partners and add important information that they might have missed on their own. Then have them cut out their wheels. Create a bulletin board titled "Motoring Toward Summarizing Success." (Standard 7.5)

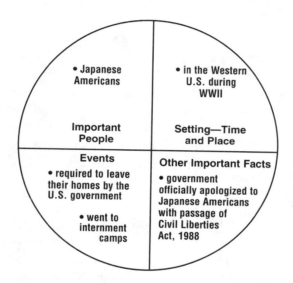

Strategy 3: Key-Word Note Taking

Key-word note taking is a great way for students to read for important information and create a study guide at the same time. Using the activity on page 238, have students record facts and other important details and definitions on the right side of the note-taking form. Then, on the left side of the form, have students identify the big ideas. Sometimes the author will provide this information for them directly in the text, but sometimes students must infer the big ideas. After students have completed the note-taking graphic organizer, show them how to use it as a study guide. Model for them how to fold the graphic organizer on the line that divides the left side and the right side. Have students quiz themselves on the facts that match the key words. Then show students how to turn the study guide over and quiz themselves on key words that match the facts. Students can work independently or with partners to study this information. One of the benefits of this technique is that it builds students' independence in mastering their own learning. (Standards 5.8, 7.5)

Summarize and Synthesize

Strategy 4: Step-by-Step Paraphrasing

Paraphrasing is a critical skill that is taught best in a step-by-step manner. Use the activity sheet (page 239) to model for students how to read information, "hide" the text, recall the information as quickly as possible by jotting down notes, and then combine the information into a summary of what's most important. Model this process for students by using short pieces of text and having students simply recall one or two bits of information. Show students how to combine the information and write in their own words, creating the paraphrase. As the students build their proficiency with this technique, give them longer and more complex pieces of text to paraphrase. (Standard 7.5)

Strategy 5: Significant Squares

Significant squares are an alternative way to have students identify the important information in text. This technique helps students develop focus questions, identify concepts and themes, find the key facts, and reflect on the information they have gained. One way to use this strategy is to have students work with a partner or in a group to use multiple texts to gather information on the same topic. Each student in the partnership reads different text information, completes the Significant Squares (page 240), and compares information by sharing the information from the graphic organizer with his or her partner. Students can then use the information they have recorded to first form a summary of the text and then combine that with prior knowledge to form a synthesis of the text. (Standards 7.5, 7.6)

Strategy 6: Concept Mapping

Concept mapping (page 241) allows students to organize the subtopics and details around the concept they are learning. Concept mapping also allows for flexibility in that students can identify different subtopics and arrange the details accordingly. It is beneficial to students to do a whole-class concept map on a topic that they are familiar with first before they use this technique with a text. Given the concept of teamwork, students might identify such subtopics as sports, school, home, and community. Within those subtopics, they would identify appropriate details. Students can use the concept map to summarize or synthesize the information surrounding each subtopic. (Standards 7.5, 7.6)

Sports

Teammates have to work together to play hard against opponents and win a game.

Teamwork

Home

Every member in a family has to pitch in and work together on chores and tasks.

School

It is important to work with your classmates on projects and activities so that you may learn from each other and learn how to cooperate with others.

Community

Members of a community must work together to improve and maintain their community.

Summarize and Synthesize

Strategy 7: Practice with Paraphrasing and Summarizing

Paraphrasing is a process. What follows is an overview of that process. You may break it down for students in manageable chunks. For example, focus only on clarifying vocabulary in one set of lessons; then move to finding the essence of a sentence. Then work on sifting out words and phrases to be avoided when paraphrasing and developing synonyms for them. The activity sheets that follow will be helpful, but students will require additional modeling and practice from the teacher.

Prepare for teaching the skill of paraphrasing by collecting a variety of sentences pulled from the students' nonfiction reading material. Include sentences that contain words that will be unfamiliar to students. The topic sentences in an article from a student magazine or even an intermediate picture book would be good sources. See the Paraphrasing Sentences activity on page 242 for examples of sentences that would make good practice. One of the first steps in being able to paraphrase a sentence is making sure that students understand all the vocabulary contained within it. Write one of your collected sentences on the board. Ask students to define any unfamiliar vocabulary words by the context, or send them to their dictionaries or glossaries. Once they can define all of the words in the sentence, they can turn their attention to rewriting it.

Here is an example of a difficult sentence for students to paraphrase:

> In the past, American Indians across the country spoke more than 600 dialects based on seven major language groups.

Students obviously need to know the word *dialect* before they can paraphrase the sentence. A dialect is the way a language is spoken in a particular place or among a particular group of people. Next, ask students to notice the essence of the sentence. In the example, this would be that American Indians spoke 600 dialects based on seven language groups. They also need to notice phrases that they should not be using. Here is the example sentence without the phrase that is not needed:

> American Indians across the country spoke more than 600 dialects based on seven major language groups.

Now students may begin thinking about ways to restate the sentence. Tell them to think about synonyms for the phrases that they need to avoid and ways to vary the sentence structure while retaining its meaning.

After students have had plenty of practice paraphrasing sentences, have them try practicing paraphrasing paragraphs. Use the activity on page 243 for practice with this strategy. The information on pages 244 and 245 can be used as reference tools to help students write effective summaries and paraphrases. Challenge students to paraphrase a letter (page 246) or select a piece of material to summarize on their own (pages 247 and 248). (Standards 5.5, 7.5, 8.16)

Summarize and Synthesize

Strategy 8: Identifying Pros and Cons

For this strategy, have students read a piece of nonfiction text and determine as many pros and cons as they can that relate to the issue. Students should then decide if they need to do further research. This can be done as a class or independently. Use the activity on page 249. (Standard 7.6)

Strategy 9: Text Coding

Having students code text information as they read is particularly effective when having them identify important information. Students can use page 250 to practice this strategy. As a variation, have students read the text, bracket important information, and write a key word or phrase that summarizes the information in the bracket. If students are not allowed to write in the text, provide them with sticky notes and instruct them to align the note with the text and write the bracket and the key word or phrase on the sticky note. (Standard 7.5)

Strategy 10: 5 Ws and How

An oldie but goodie, the 5 Ws and How strategy can really help students focus on what's important. Students can use the double-entry journal for 5 Ws and How (page 251) to record key information from the text and write a summary using this information. Another way to have students use this strategy is to divide students into groups of four to six and assign each member of the group one of the 5 Ws and How. In this way they can focus on one element of the text as they are reading. Have them fill out a graphic organizer together when they are finished reading and share their information. (Standard 7.5)

The 5 Ws and How	A Summary from the 5 Ws and How
Who: Harriet Tubman **What:** was the famous leader of the Underground Railroad **Where:** in states where slavery was legal **When:** the 1850s **Why:** to help slaves escape to freedom **How:** with the help of a secret network of sympathetic people who wanted to free slaves	Harriet Tubman was the famous leader of the Underground Railroad. In the 1850s, she helped slaves escape from states where slavery was legal. She worked with a secret network of sympathetic people who wanted to help free slaves.

Strategy 11: Before/During/After Note Taking

Teaching students that note taking is a process, just like reading and writing are processes, can be very helpful. Before students begin reading, have them use the graphic organizer on page 252 to preview, predict, and question. As they read, the organizer guides them to read, pause, and identify important information. After they are finished reading, students will reflect on what they have learned, link new information to old information, and think of ways that they can retain the information they have gained. (Standard 5.1)

Summarize and Synthesize

Note-Taking Wheel

Directions: Use the following graphic organizer to take notes on significant information. When taking notes, remember to:

- ❏ **Use short phrases, not complete sentences.**
- ❏ **Use your own words.**
- ❏ **Write quickly; don't worry about handwriting, spelling, or grammar.**
- ❏ **Use abbreviations when possible.**

| Important People | Setting—Time and Place |
| Events | Other Important Facts |

Summarize and Synthesize

Key-Word Note Taking

Directions: Use the following graphic organizer to record the key words (big ideas, major categories, main ideas) in the left-hand column. Record the related details and facts in the right-hand column. Use this sheet as a study guide by folding the paper to hide the key words. Then quiz yourself by reading the details and facts and remembering the key words associated with the factual information.

Key word (big idea or major category of information)	Related details and facts
	1. 2.
	1. 2.
	1. 2.
	1. 2.

Summarize and Synthesize

Step-by-Step Paraphrasing

Step 1: Read the text information and think about the main ideas and supporting details.

Step 2: Reread if necessary.

Step 3: Close the textbook or turn the text over so that you can't see any of the words. As quickly as possible, jot down as many important things as you can remember in the box below. This will be your summary. Remember to write quickly, use abbreviations if possible, and don't worry about spelling, punctuation, or grammar.

Notes:

Step 4: Look back over your notes and highlight or underline the most important information. Use your summary to paraphrase what you read in the space provided below. Remember, you are using your own words to relate the most important information from the text.

_____

_____

_____

_____

_____

_____

_____

_____

Summarize and Synthesize

Significant Squares

Directions: Before reading, generate a list of questions to guide you toward the significant information. As you read, identify key concepts/themes and important facts. After reading, identify how you know when information is important.

Focus questions before reading	Key concepts and themes
Important facts learned	**Reflection: How do I know when information is important?**

Summarize and Synthesize

Concept Mapping

Directions: Record the key concept in the center box. Then record the subtopics in the outer boxes and relevant details on the lines provided for you.

Summarize and Synthesize

Paraphrasing Sentences

Directions: Read each proverb below and discuss its meaning with your classmates. Then paraphrase the proverbs. Paraphrasing proverbs and sayings can provide good practice with summarizing. Remember that to paraphrase means to rewrite another author's words in your own words while still keeping the author's meaning.

1. A penny saved is a penny earned. _____

2. You can catch more flies with honey than with vinegar. _____
   _____

3. The only thing certain in life is death and taxes. _____
   _____

4. Finders, keepers; losers, weepers. _____

5. Make hay while the sun shines. _____

6. Birds of a feather flock together. _____

7. Let sleeping dogs lie. _____

8. All's well that ends well. _____

9. Don't count your chickens before they hatch. _____

10. Haste makes waste. _____

11. An apple a day keeps the doctor away. _____

12. Great minds think alike. _____

13. Too many cooks spoil the broth. _____

14. A watched pot never boils. _____

15. A stitch in time saves nine. _____

16. Loose lips sink ships. _____

17. A journey of a thousand miles begins with a single step. _____
    _____

18. You can lead a horse to water, but you can't make it drink. _____
    _____

19. Home is where the heart is. _____

20. Beauty is in the eye of the beholder. _____

Summarize and Synthesize

Paraphrasing Paragraphs

Directions: Rewriting paragraphs in your own words takes a lot of thought. Remember that you need to understand the vocabulary words in each sentence and that you should avoid repeating the author's phrasing. Also, think about synonyms for the words and phrases the author used. Read the paragraphs below; then rewrite them in your own words on a separate sheet of paper. Use your own language and your own way of expressing thoughts.

Paragraph I

It takes a very special person to be an astronaut. An astronaut must be in excellent health and physical shape. He or she must be a good learner and do well in math and science and be able to solve problems calmly, quickly, and logically. An astronaut needs self-confidence and the will to succeed—and he or she must be a team player, able to work well with others to meet a goal.

Paragraph 2

Labor Day is a special holiday that honors working people by giving them a day off work to rest on the first Monday in September. In the past, the working conditions of many jobs were very poor. Workers sometimes worked 12–14 hours a day for six or seven days a week, with little pay and in hazardous or unhealthy conditions. At times, even very young children of six or seven had to work 10-hour days to help their families survive.

Paragraph 3

The eagle has long been a symbol of strength and power. Countries and even empires have chosen the eagle as their symbol. So when it came time to choose a national bird for America, many wanted it to be the eagle. But not everyone agreed. Benjamin Franklin proposed that the turkey be the national bird because it was a true native of the new country. However, in 1782, the Congress chose the bald eagle, a bird also unique to North America, but perhaps a more fitting symbol for a strong and brave new nation.

Summarize and Synthesize

How to Write a Summary

A summary is a condensed, or short, version of a paragraph, chapter, article, or book. Summaries can serve several purposes. They can simply retell descriptive or chronological information or give a brief rundown of a process. They also can give an overview of an author's argument with the author's main idea and important points.

When you write a summary, you will need to do quite a bit of thinking. You will need to think about the author's main idea and the supporting details. You will also need to know how to paraphrase, or rewrite, the author's words in as brief a form as possible.

Summaries can be as short as a sentence or as long as a page or two, depending on the length of the material that you need to summarize.

Here are the seven steps to writing a summary:

Step 1. Read the material carefully.

Think about the main idea of what you are reading. Notice the most important supporting details or facts. Make sure that you understand the author's argument or conclusion.

Step 2. Reread the material.

As you read, think about the type of text it is. Also use the text organizers, such as subheadings, to help you organize your thinking about the material. You want to include information from each section of what you read. You may want to jot down any important points or key words and phrases that you would like to include in your summary.

Step 3. Write the main idea.

This will help you stay focused on the information to include in your summary.

Step 4. Write summary sentences.

Write sentences that tell about each section of what you read.

Step 5. Write a draft of your summary.

Look over the main idea, key words and phrases, and sentences that you wrote. Now write a summary that gives the basic information that the reader needs to know. You do not need to include all the supporting details in your summary. Just tell the reader a few of the most important facts.

Step 6. Check your information.

Look over the original material that you read. Did you include only the most important points? Did you leave out anything that the reader should know?

Step 7. Rewrite your summary.

Read your work. It should read smoothly. Use the transition words from the chart on page 245 to help you.

Summarize and Synthesize

Useful Phrases for Paraphrasing and Summarizing

When paraphrasing and summarizing ideas, it can be helpful to remember certain transitional words and phrases. The words and phrases in the chart below can help take the reader from one thought to another. They can help say more with fewer words, too. In addition, these words and phrases can help writers organize summaries, especially when they are summarizing a longer piece of work.

Summarizing a Topic

and so	in all	in summary	this shows
briefly	in brief	that is	to conclude
finally	in other words	therefore	to sum up
generally	in short		

Comparing Topics

also	by comparison	likewise	similarly
as	here again	moreover	so too
as well	in the same way		

Contrasting Topics

although	even though	on the other hand	still
anyhow	however	otherwise	yet
but	instead of		

To Show Cause and Effect

accordingly	hence	then	thereupon
as a result	it follows that	therefore	thus
for this reason			

To Explain

actually	for instance	namely	such as
because	in fact	of course	that is
for example	in this way	since	

To Add Information

add to this	and	in addition	too
again	as well	next	yet again
also	besides	then too	

To Show Chronological Order

after that	by that time	first, second, etc.	next
afterwards	during	in the end	now
at last	earlier	in the meantime	soon
before that	finally	later	then

Summarize and Synthesize

Paraphrase a Letter

Directions: Jane wants to send a letter home telling her family and friends about all the interesting facts that she discovered on her vacation. However, she does not want to copy the same long letter over and over again. She decides to send postcards instead. How can Jane summarize her letter so that it fits on the postcard below?

Dear Family and Friends,

This week we traveled up and down the coast of California and saw many wonderful sights. We went to the Aerospace Museum in San Diego, the Getty Museum in Los Angeles, and the Exploratorium Science Museum in San Francisco. We went to a small zoo in Santa Barbara and a big aquarium in Monterey. We ate Thai food, Mexican food, Italian food, and Chinese food. We saw a lot of different landmarks, including the Golden Gate Bridge and Alcatraz in San Francisco.

We learned a great deal about California history, too. Did you know that the missions were built just far enough apart to be reached by horseback in a day? Or that the Presidio was a military post for Spain, then Mexico, and finally the United States? I also learned that it was not the earthquake, but the fires caused by it, that ruined the city of San Francisco.

I can't wait to show you my photographs when I return.

Sincerely,

Jane

Summarize and Synthesize

Writing a Summary—Part 1

Directions: Choose one of the following types of material to summarize. How brief can you make your summaries and still tell your reader the most important information? Write your summaries on a separate page.

1. Encyclopedia article on your favorite animal

2. Documentary film or program on a subject you enjoy

3. Nonfiction book on a topic that interests you

4. Chapter from a science textbook

5. Editorial from a newspaper

6. Article from a science magazine

7. Nonfiction picture book

8. Encyclopedia article on your favorite place

9. Article from a Web site

10. Classroom or school newsletter

11. Recipe from a cookbook

12. Article about your favorite sports figure

13. Article from a popular magazine

14. How-to book

15. Article on a health or medical topic

16. Chapter from a social studies textbook

17. Encyclopedia article on a famous military person

18. Nonfiction book about a historical period

19. Encyclopedia article on a famous artist

20. Nonfiction book about a celebration or festival

Summarize and Synthesize

Writing a Summary—Part 2

Directions: Identify the topic and the details from the text and then use the information to write a concise summary.

Topic:

Details:
 	
  1.
 	
  2.
 	
  3.

Writing a Summary: Use the information above to write a summary that clearly includes the most important information from the text. Remember:

➤ Include the important facts in your own words.

➤ Combine facts where possible.

➤ Exclude extra information.

_____

_____

_____

_____

_____

_____

_____

_____

_____

Summarize and Synthesize

Identifying Pros and Cons

Directions: Read the text and determine as many pros and cons as you can that are related to the issue. Before you identify your opinion of the topic or issue, decide if you need to do any further research and gather more information. You may need to go to the library to get the information you need.

Major Issue: _____

Pros
Cons
Further Research
Your Opinion

Summarize and Synthesize

Text Coding

Directions: Use the following codes to identify important information while reading. Mark your codes directly in the margin of the text, use a sticky note, or make a bookmark. After reading, choose one of the codes and copy the related text information in the left-hand column of the chart. Then reflect on the significance of the information in the right-hand column of the chart. Use the sentence starters to help begin your reflections.

I = Important information

Wow! = Extremely surprising information

F = Fact

O = Opinion

C = Concept or "big idea"

Text information	Reflection (sentence starters)
Code____	This information surprised me because…
Code____	This fact/opinion is important because…
Code____	I know this is a "big idea" because…
Code____	Coding text information helped me because…

Summarize and Synthesize

Using the 5 Ws and How

Directions: Read the text and identify the 5 Ws and How on the left-hand side of the double-entry journal. Then write a summary on the right-hand side of the double-entry journal.

The 5 Ws and How	Write a summary using the 5 Ws and How
Who:	
What:	
Where:	
When:	
Why:	
How:	

Summarize and Synthesize

Before/During/After Note Taking

Directions: Use the following graphic organizer to take notes before, during, and after reading.

❑ Preview the text and look at the headings, subheadings, bold words, and italicized words.

❑ What do you predict will be the important information?

❑ What questions do you have?

❑ Read the text information carefully.

❑ Pause throughout your reading to think about your predictions.

❑ As you read, identify the main ideas and details in the space below. Write the main ideas in all capital letters so as to differentiate them from the details.

❑ Take a moment to reflect on what you have learned.

❑ Link new information to your prior knowledge about the topic.

❑ Answer the question: How will I remember this information?

PASSPORT TO COMPREHENSION

Developing Vocabulary

Developing Vocabulary

Introduction

Most instructors know that rote memorization of vocabulary words is ineffective for expanding students' word knowledge. Yet, students need to understand new words that they encounter in their reading if their knowledge base is going to increase. In addition to learning word meanings in context, students also need skills to break words down in order to approach their reading with independence and confidence.

Nonfiction reading, especially, requires the ability to understand technical language. Science and social studies demand that students recognize and build their vocabulary. Mathematics also has a specialized language that students must learn if they are to advance.

Teaching vocabulary can be a frustrating experience if you do not have a plan other than assigning a list of words for students to define in the glossary or dictionary as homework. Allot instructional time to word study. Students need to learn not only the meanings of words, but also their applicability. In other words, once students learn a new term, they can think about other contexts in which the term might be used and in this way enlarge their schema about that term. When beginning to read a rich chapter or book, it is easy to be lured into diving into the material. Time spent on word study at the outset, however, will pay off handsomely as students will better comprehend the material and begin to use the vocabulary independently. In short, Abbott (1999) states that vocabulary development should help students:

- become adept at using a variety of word recognition strategies
- unlock meanings of technical and specialized words in each content area
- establish a systematic, lifelong method of vocabulary inquiry
- become motivated and enthusiastic about vocabulary study

Strategies for Teaching Vocabulary in Context

There are many ways to approach vocabulary instruction; some are more comprehensive than others. Choose strategies based upon the difficulty of the language encountered and the amount of emphasis you wish to place in a particular content area. For example, teaching the vocabulary of art and teaching the vocabulary of science will require different approaches. Maintain flexibility and be open-minded. Most of all, approach word study with enthusiasm.

Strategy 1: Predicting Text

Predicting text is an important skill. Readers read faster and with better comprehension if they are able to predict what the author will say. The activities on pages 259 and 260 have sentences with an entire word missing or with the missing word's first and last letters added as clues. Both variations offer students excellent opportunities to practice this strategy. (Standard 5.3)

Developing Vocabulary

Strategy 2: Using Context to Understand New Words

One effective strategy for students to use when tackling unknown vocabulary words is learning how to define words in context. When reading, students can gain a sense of context from the sentence or paragraph that contains the word. Students also gain context through a clear sense of the concept they are exploring, the topics they are studying, and the purpose for their learning. The broad educational picture combined with the text itself gives students context through which to make meaning of unknown words. Structured discussion, small-group dialogue, and paired readings can also give students an idea of context as they hear the teacher and their classmates use unknown words in real-life conversations. When proficient readers encounter a word they don't know, they ask three questions:

1. Do I know this word?

2. If so, how do I know this word? If not, how can I know this word?

3. Do I need to know this word?

Proficient readers answer these questions by using context, activating prior knowledge, and using resources available to them. Struggling readers have great difficulty using context and will need highly structured word attack strategies in order to make sense of unknown words. Use the activity on page 261 to practice this strategy. (Standards 5.5, 7.6)

Strategy 3: Important Word Parts in English—Roots/Prefixes/Suffixes

One of the main reasons for the high gains in vocabulary knowledge in children is their growing awareness and proficiency with root words, suffixes, and prefixes. Morphology is the ability to use word structures to make meaning of new vocabulary. Explicit instruction that teaches students how to use their prior knowledge to make sense of root words, suffixes, and prefixes will result in growing confidence levels in understanding words and, ultimately, an increase in reading comprehension. A list of the most important word parts in English is given on page 262 for students to use. Use the activity on page 263 to have students chart unknown words, definitions, roots, prefixes, and suffixes. The following are some key questions that will help students with using morphology. (Standards 5.4, 7.6)

1. What is the root word? What prior knowledge do I have to help me define this word?

2. What is the prefix? What does it mean? How does it change the root word?

3. What is the suffix? What does it mean? How does it change the root word?

4. How does knowing parts of words help me to understand the meanings of new words?

Strategy 4: Latin Word Parts and Prefix Circles

Many words in the English language use Latin roots. Students can become independent readers when they recognize and tuck away the meanings of these Latin root words. Use pages 264 and 265 to initiate awareness of Latin root words. Keep a running list posted in the classroom. Assign prefix circles (page 266) to stimulate students to think about these important word parts. (Standard 5.4)

Developing Vocabulary

Strategy 5: Synonyms and Antonyms

Students should make a list of unknown words from the text they are reading. Then they can look up each of the words and write definitions for them. Using the definitions, students should think of synonyms and antonyms for each of the words. This will help students make connections with the text instead of merely thinking of the words in isolation. Use page 267 for practice. (Standards 5.4, 5.7)

Strategy 6: Dictionary Definitions

Oftentimes, students need practice using a dictionary to look up unknown words. Using the activity on page 268, have students make a list of words that they need to know the meanings of. Then have students look up the words and make note of the guide words at the top of the pages, the pronunciation of the words, the parts of speech, and the definitions. (Standard 5.4)

Strategy 7: Artistic Definitions

A great way to build students' understanding of new words is to use art and drama. Use the Artistic Definitions activity page (page 269) to have students identify the unknown word, define it in context, and then use a dictionary. Instruct students to draw an illustration of the word interacting with other ideas, people, places, or things. For example, if the word is "freedom," a student may draw a picture of a happy woman or man holding hands with the American flag, the Statue of Liberty, and a bald eagle— all symbols of freedom in our country. Such a picture would show that the student understood cultural synonyms for the word "freedom" and knew how to express the relationship between the word and these synonyms through art. (Standard 5.5)

Strategy 8: Conceptual Definitions

Students consider how a concept relates to other ideas that they are studying. Using the activity on page 270, students think about a vocabulary concept and four major subcategories of this concept. Then students record details about each of the subcategories to show how they relate to the main idea. (Standard 7.5)

Strategy 9: Word Origins

The study of the English language is fascinating because it draws from so many different sources. Keep some reference books in the classroom that provide a history of the English language and word origins. Using word origins is a colorful way to add interest to vocabulary study. Use the activity on page 271 to stimulate an initial discussion. (Standards 5.4, 8.16)

Strategy 10: Vocabulary Questioning

Have students use a chart to answer questions about vocabulary words that they are studying in order to develop a deeper understanding of them. They will answer questions about how the word connects to a personal experience, to other words, to sensory details, and to similes and metaphors, as well as how it is useful. They will also give examples of the word. Use the activity on page 272. (Standards 7.6, 8.15)

Developing Vocabulary

Strategy 11: Word Categorization Chart

One way to organize vocabulary study is to create a categorization chart of terms. Carefully pre-read the text and pull out the important terms; then organize them in such a way that the terms are categorized. For example, here is a list of terms related to volcanoes:

core	gases	avalanche
magma	crust	mantle
eruption	lava	tsunami

Here are the terms organized into categories:

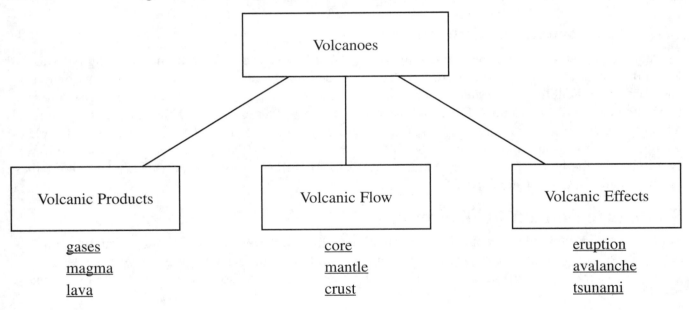

Have students use the activity on page 273 to practice organizing terms. Once students understand the process that you used to create such a chart, invite them to create their own charts of terms. Such charts can facilitate recall of definitions because all of the vocabulary is linked in a logical, contextual way. Use the organizer on page 274. (Standard 5.4)

Strategy 12: Word Study Cards

When you are working on a particularly long unit of study, word cards can be a good way for students to keep track of important new vocabulary. You may wish to make transparencies of page 275 to demonstrate how to complete the cards when you introduce them. You can require all students to keep track of the same words or allow individual students to choose terms unfamiliar to them. Students can use the cards to help them prepare for quizzes and exams and also refer to them when writing summaries and reports. (Standard 5.4)

Developing Vocabulary

Predicting Text—Part 1

Directions: Read aloud the following sentences, substituting "Hmmm" for the blank. Ask the students to write the word that would finish each sentence. Accept any sensible answers. Do about five each day until students demonstrate competence. At first you may need to read these sentences twice to ensure students' success, but move to a singular reading as soon as possible.

1. We live on the continent called _____.

2. The country to the north of the United States is _____.

3. Animals must eat either plants or other _____.

4. Twelve minus four is _____.

5. The ocean we live the closest to is called the _____ Ocean.

6. A tall, often rocky land form is called a _____.

7. Eight plus six is _____.

8. She said that the outside temperature was 36 _____.

9. Wood is an example of the _____ form of matter.

10. When you subtract _____ from any number, the number stays the same.

11. The first president of our country, _____, lived at Mount Vernon.

12. When you cut a finger, _____ comes out of the wound.

13. To stop cavities from forming, you should _____ your teeth.

14. Water is an example of the _____ form of matter.

15. We have _____ senses.

16. When you add _____ to any number, the number stays the same.

17. Some examples of _____ are bears, rabbits, dolphins, and seals.

18. A _____ is an animal you can find in the desert.

19. A _____ is a mountain that gives off smoke, ashes, and lava.

20. _____ makes lamps light up and appliances work.

21. A _____ is a coin worth 25 cents.

22. A _____ has four equal sides.

23. _____ are cold-blooded animals.

24. A _____ has three sides.

25. _____ flashes in the sky during a thunderstorm.

Developing Vocabulary

Predicting Text—Part 2

Directions: Have students write a word that would best complete each sentence. Spelling does not count. Initial and final letters are given to help students attend to visual cues in addition to context. Do about five of these a day.

1. Over time tadpoles turn into f_____ s.

2. Clouds can bring snow or r _____ n.

3. A baby bear is called a c _____ b.

4. Red is a primary c _____ r.

5. The continent at the South Pole is A _____ a.

6. The world's biggest ocean is the P _____ c.

7. Abraham Lincoln set slaves f _____ e in 1863.

8. To find the spelling of a word, look it up in the d _____ y.

9. There are 12 m _____ s in a year.

10. There are 365 d _____ s in a year.

11. Clouds are made of w _____ r vapor.

12. During the day, the s _____ n shines on Earth.

13. Mexico is the c _____ y to the south of the United States.

14. Four q _____ s make a dollar.

15. There are f _____ r seasons.

16. On July 4, 1776, we declared our i _____ e from Britain.

17. A 90-degree angle is called a r _____ t angle.

18. F _____ y comes after January.

19. A n _____ l is a coin worth five cents.

20. G _____ n is a secondary color.

21. The P _____ s came to America to have religious freedom.

22. T _____ e are seven continents on Earth.

23. Y _____ u use your teeth to chew your food.

24. T _____ s and cars stop when the light is red.

25. A r _____ e has four right angles.

Developing Vocabulary

Using Context to Understand New Words

Directions: Read each sentence. Use the clues for each sentence (see symbols below) to help you figure out what each underlined word means.

*	The meaning is given somewhere else in the sentence or paragraph.
+	Find the meaning by looking for a contrast word such as "but."
#	The meaning is not directly stated.

*1. A foul, <u>offensive</u> odor was coming from the box in the corner.

The word *offensive* means _____.

#2. It was <u>ridiculous</u> to expect Dr. Line to go along with such a crazy idea.

The word *ridiculous* means _____.

+3. I didn't want to go into the <u>crypt</u>, but I didn't want to stand out in the dark graveyard, either.

The word *crypt* means _____.

*4. Barn owls like to eat <u>voles</u>—mice-like animals with stubby tails.

The word *voles* means _____.

#5. If they stay away from <u>predators</u>, sea horses can live up to three years.

The word *predators* means _____.

+6. Unlike Susan, who was always <u>prompt</u>, Jack was never on time.

The word *prompt* means _____.

*7. The <u>biologist</u>, a scientist who studies living things, does research on plants and animals.

The word *biologist* means _____.

+8. Most metals rust, but gold does not <u>corrode</u>.

The word *corrode* means _____.

*9. Arlington National <u>Cemetery</u>, or graveyard, is where we bury our national heroes.

The word *cemetery* means _____.

Developing Vocabulary

Important Word Parts in English

Prefix	Meaning	Root	Meaning	Suffix	Meaning
un-	not	act	do	-s or -es	more than one
re-	again	ast	star	-ed	verb ending
in-, im-	not	cycl	circle	-ing	verb ending
dis-	opposite	fac	make, do	-ly	like, every
en-, em-	in	form	shape	-er, -or	one who
non-	not	gram	letter, written	-ition, -ation	state or quality of
over-	too much	graph	write	-able, -ible	inclined to, apt to
mis-	bad	man	hand	-al, -ial	relating to
sub-	below	meter	measure	-ness	state or quality of
pre-	before	bio	life	-ity, -ty	state or quality of
inter-	among, between	geo	earth	-ment	action or product
fore-	before, in front	ped	foot	-ic	system
de-	opposite	phon	sound	-ous, -ious	state or quality of
trans-	across	photo	light	-en	relating to
super-	over, more than	port	carry	-er	more (comparative)
semi-	partial, half	scope	see	-tive, -sive, -ive	inclined to, apt to
anti-	against	spect	see	-ful	full of
mid-	middle	struct	build, form	-less	without
under-	too little	therm	heat	-est	most (comparative)

Prefixes and suffixes are from White, T., et.al. "Teaching Elementary Students to Use Word-Part Clues," *The Reading Teacher* 42, (1989): 302–309.

Roots were selected from Fry, E., et.al. *The Reading Teacher's Book of Lists*. (Jossey-Bass, 2000).

Developing Vocabulary

Roots/Prefixes/Suffixes

Directions: Identify the unknown words in the text that you have been assigned. Look up and record the definitions, roots, prefixes, and suffixes.

Unknown Word	Definition	Root	Prefixes	Suffixes

Developing Vocabulary

Latin Word Parts

Directions: Use the chart below as a reference when trying to understand new words. In time, you will become familiar with these word parts, and you will be able to read more independently.

Latin root	Definition	Example words
ambi	both, around	ambidextrous, ambiguous
ante	before, prior to	antecedent, ancestor
brev	short	brevity, abbreviate
circum	around, about, surrounding	circumference, circumstance
contra	against	contradict, contrast
en, em	in, within	enter, embarrass, embrace
extra	outside of, beyond	extraordinary, extravagant
inter, intel	between, among	international, intellect
magn	great, large	magnify, magnificent
mal	bad, ill, wrong	malice, malignant
multi	many	multiply, multimillionaire
neg, non	not, opposite	nonsense, negative, nonbeliever
post	after, behind, later	postpone, posterior
pre	before, in front of	prejudice, preface
retro	backward, back	retroactive, retrospect
sub	under, below, lower in rank	subterranean, subtract
super	above, over, greater	supersonic, superior, supervise
trans	over, across, beyond, through	transfer, transcontinental
ultra	beyond, excessive	ultraviolet, ultrasound
medi	middle	medium, mediate
numer	number	numerical, numerous
tot	all, whole	total, totalitarian
semi	half, partly, twice	semicircle, semiannual
uni, prim	one, first	uniform, primary, unite

Developing Vocabulary

Latin Word Parts (cont.)

Latin root	Definition	Example words
cord	heart	cordial, discord
capit	head	capital, captain
ped	foot	biped, pedal
manu, mani	hand	manual, manicure
aud	hear	audible, audio
ocul	eye	binoculars, ocular
digit	finger, toe	digital, digit
corpor	body	corpse, corporation
dent	tooth	dental, dentist, indent
ora	mouth, speak, prayer	oral, oracle, adoration
terr	earth, land	territory, terrace, terrain
sol	sun	solar, solarium
lun	moon	lunar, lunatic
mar	sea	marina, marine, mariner
mater, matr	mother	maternal, matron
pater, patr	father	paternal, patron
frater	brother	fraternal, fraternity
soror	sister	sorority
fili	son, daughter	filial, affiliation
arbor	tree	arbor, arboretum
flor	flower	floral, florist
fol	leaf	foliage, folio
agr	field	agriculture, agrarian
aqua	water	aquarium, aqueduct
habit	dwell	inhabit, habitat

Developing Vocabulary

Prefix Circles

Directions: How many words can you think of that use the root words in the middle of each web? One has been started for you. When you are finished, create prefix circles for a partner to complete.

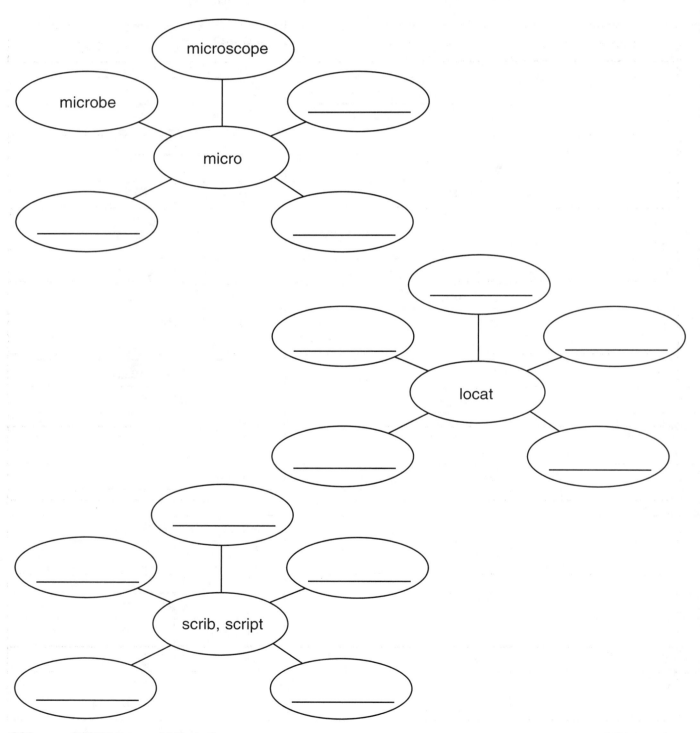

Developing Vocabulary

Synonyms and Antonyms

Directions: Identify the unknown word, look up and record the definition, and use the definition to think of synonyms and antonyms.

Unknown word	Definition	Synonyms	Antonyms

Developing Vocabulary

Dictionary Definitions

Directions: Use the dictionary to complete the following exercise regarding unknown vocabulary words.

Unknown word	Guide words at top of page	Pronunciation	Part of speech	Definition

Developing Vocabulary

Artistic Definitions

Directions: Identify the unknown word and use the context to write a definition. After looking up the word in a dictionary, draw a creative picture of the word. Finally, reflect on your drawing by responding to the questions at the bottom of the page.

Unknown word: _____

Definition based on context: _____

_____

Dictionary definition: _____

_____

Illustration of the word: (Draw a picture that shows the word interacting with other people, places, or things. Be creative!)

```




```

What details did you add to your picture that surprised you? What are your most creative or insightful details?

_____

_____

_____

How did drawing a picture of the word help you to better understand the word?

_____

_____

_____

Developing Vocabulary

Conceptual Definitions

Directions: Record the concept that you are learning in the center oval. Identify major subcategories and record them in the outer boxes. List details that describe the subcategories in the lines under each box.

Developing Vocabulary

Word Origins

Directions: The words below have an interesting origin, or history. Using a variety of resources, write the origin of each word; then write a sentence that demonstrates that you understand the word's meaning.

1. nickname _____
   _____

2. jeans _____
   _____

3. shampoo _____
   _____

4. city _____
   _____

5. antler _____
   _____

6. travel _____
   _____

7. varmint_____
   _____

8. kindergarten _____
   _____

9. tunnel_____
   _____

10. candy_____
    _____

11. atlas_____
    _____

12. lantern _____
    _____

13. pupil_____
    _____

14. robot _____
    _____

15. toxic_____
    _____

Developing Vocabulary

Vocabulary Questioning

Directions: Use the following chart to answer questions about the vocabulary word that you are studying in order to develop a deeper understanding of it.

Vocabulary Word or Concept: _____

How does this vocabulary word connect to my personal experience?	Why do I need to know this word? How will it be useful to me?
How does this word connect to other words that I am learning related to this topic?	What similes or metaphors could I create using this word?
What sensory details connect to this word?	What are some examples of this word?

Developing Vocabulary

Word Categorization Chart—Part 1

Directions: Categorize the following words, placing the main categories in the boxes, and the terms that belong with each category on the lines below it.

mineral	palm	vegetable	animal
sunflower	titanium	monkey	sulfur
fern	diamond	armadillo	gazelle

_____	_____	_____

_____   _____   _____

_____   _____   _____

_____   _____   _____

Directions: Categorize the following words; then add terms of your own to complete the chart below. You may refer to resources such as the dictionary or the Internet.

oregano	marjoram	jasmine	vines
lobelia	vinca	Indian hawthorn	herbs

_____	_____	_____

_____   _____   _____

_____   _____   _____

_____   _____   _____

Developing Vocabulary

Word Categorization Chart—Part 2

Directions: Use the organizer below to help you categorize vocabulary terms that you need to know in order to understand your current reading.

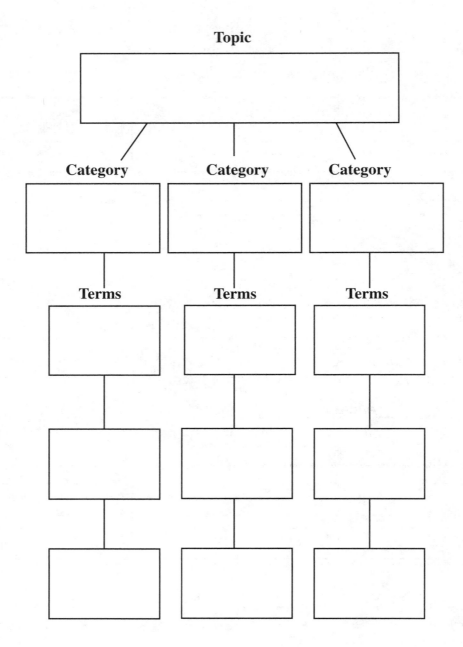

Developing Vocabulary

Word Study Cards

Directions: Complete the word study card below for each word that you must know in order to understand a chapter, article, or book. The top one has been done for you as an example.

Term: diversity

Definition: a variety

Elaboration: Many things can be diverse, such as people, birds, insects, and types of cooking.

Connections: Our classroom is diverse because we have students from all over the world.

Synonyms: varied, different, multiple, many

Antonyms: unvaried, unified, single, one

Example sentence: I have learned a great deal about different cultures because of the diversity of students in our classroom.

Term: _____

Definition: _____

Elaboration: _____

Connections: _____

Synonyms: _____

Antonyms: _____

Example sentence: _____

Works Cited

Abbott, S. 1999. *Teaching reading in the middle grades*. Huntington Beach, CA: Teacher Created Materials, Inc.

Baker, L. 2002. Metacognition in comprehension instruction. In *Comprehension Instruction: Research-based best practices*, ed. C. C. Block and M. Pressley, 77–95. New York: The Guilford Press.

Baker, L., and A. L. Brown. 1984. Metacognitive skills and reading. In *Handbook of reading research*, ed. P. D. Pearson, R. Barr, M. L. Kamil, and P. Mosenthal, 353–394. Mahwah, NJ: Lawrence Erlbaum.

Block, C. C. 1999. Comprehension: Crafting understanding. In *Best practices in literacy instruction*, ed. L. B. Gambrell, L. M. Morrow, S. B. Neuman, and M. Pressley, 98–118. New York: Guilford Press.

Dole, J. A., K. J. Brown, and W. Trathen. 1996. The effects of strategy instruction on the comprehension performance of at-risk students. *Reading Research Quarterly* 31:62–88.

Duke, N. K., and P. D. Pearson. 2002. Effective practices for developing reading comprehension. In *What research has to say about reading instruction*. 3rd ed. Ed. A. E. Farstup and S. J. Samuels, 205–242. Newark, DE: International Reading Association, Inc.

Durkin, D. 1978. What classroom observations reveal about reading comprehension instruction. *Reading Research Quarterly* 14:481–538.

Enciso, P. 1992. Creating the storyworld: A case study of a young reader's engagement strategies and stances. In *Reader stance and literary understanding: Exploring the theories, research, and practice*, ed. J. Many and C. Cox, 75–102. Norwood, NJ: Ablex.

Garner, R. 1987. *Metacognition and reading comprehension*. Norwood, NJ: Ablex.

Irvin, J. L. 1998. *Reading and the middle school student: Strategies to enhance literacy.* Needham Heights, MA: Allyn and Bacon.

Keene, E. O. 2002. From good to memorable: Characteristics of highly effective comprehension teaching. In *Improving comprehension instruction*, ed. C. C. Block, L. B. Gambrell, and M. Pressley, 80–105. San Francisco: Jossey-Bass.

Kragler, S., C. A. Walker, and L. E. Martin. 2005. Strategy instruction in primary content textbooks. *The Reading Teacher* 59 (3): 254–261.

Langer, J. 1987. Envisionment: A reader-based view of comprehension. *The California Reader* 20 (3): 4–7.

Mastropieri, M. A., and T. E. Scruggs. 1997. Best practices in promoting reading comprehension in students with learning disabilities. *Remedial and Special Education* 18 (4): 197–214.

Works Cited

McCarthy, S., L. Hoffman, and J. Galda. 1999. Readers in elementary classrooms: Learning goals and instructional principles. In *Engaged reading*, ed. J. Guthrie, and D. Alvermann, 46–80. New York: Teachers College Press.

Meichenbaum, D., B. Burland, L. Gruson, and R. Cameron. 1985. The growth of reflection in children. In *Metacognitive Assessment*, ed. S. Yusson, 3–30. London: Academic Press.

National Reading Panel. 2000. *Teaching children to read: An evidence-based assessment of the scientific research literature on reading and its implications for reading instruction—reports of the subgroups.* Washington, DC: National Institute of Child Health and Human Development.

Paris, S. G., B. A. Wasik, and J. C. Turner. 1991. The development of strategic readers. In vol. 2 of *Handbook of reading research,* ed. R. Barr, M. L. Kamil, P. Mosenthal, and P. D. Pearson, 609–640. Mahwah, NJ: Lawrence Erlbaum.

Pressley, M. 2000. What should comprehension instruction be the instruction of? In vol. 3 of *Handbook of reading research,* ed. R. Barr, M. L. Kamil, P. B. Mosenthal, and P. D. Pearson, 545–562. Mahwah, NJ: Lawrence Erlbaum Associates, Inc.

———. 2002. Metacognition and self-regulated comprehension. In *What reasearch has to say about reading instruction.* 3rd ed. Ed. A. E. Farstrup and S. J. Samuels, 291–309. Newark, DE: International Reading Association, Inc.

Pressley, M., and P. Afflerbach. 1995. *Verbal protocols for reading: The nature of constructively responsive reading.* Hillsdale, NJ: Lawrence Erlbaum.

Raphael, T., and K. Au. 2005. QAR: Enhancing comprehension and test taking across grades and content areas. *The Reading Teacher* 59 (3): 206–221.

Robinson, F. P. 1970. *Effective study.* 4th ed. New York: Harper and Row.

Roehler, L. R., and G. G. Duffy. 1991. Teacher's instructional actions. In vol. 2 of *Handbook of reading research,* ed. R. Barr, M. L. Kamil, P. B. Mosenthal, and P. D. Pearson, 861–884. White Plains: Longman.

Schraw, G. 1998. Promoting general metacognitive awareness. *Instructional Science* 26:113–125

Notes

Notes

Notes